Helping People Change

Helping People Involved in
Change, Loss and Bereavement

Bryce Taylor

Oasis Human Relation Development Organisation Ltd.

Published by
Oasis Human Relation Development Organisation Ltd.,
Hall Mews, Clifford Road, Boston Spa, West Yorkshire. LS23 6DT

TAYLOR, BRYCE 1946
Helping People Change
1. TRAINING
2. PSYCHOLOGY
 ISBN 1 871992 10 9

Printed by Maxiprint (York) Ltd., Kettlestring Lane, Clifton Moor, York, England.
Cover designed by Simon Kaye, Lowgate Studio.

Preface

This book is dedicated to helpers.

It is dedicated to all those people who at some time in their lives find themselves in the role of helper. This will not always be as professional counsellors or in a formal 'counselling relationship'. It will often arise out of family or friendship relationships. It may be in crisis, short or long term but whatever the circumstances or causes, many of us find ourselves plunged into a helping role.

Whilst there are those who do have a very valuable professional role in helping the bereaved, this book is designed to be accesssible to all individuals interested in and involved in helping those undergoing loss, change or bereavement.

Acknowledgements

I wish to thank the many people who have helped in any way to the creation of 'Helping People Change'. Those who have inspired me, clients who have permitted me to travel alongside them, clients who have allowed me to use their experiences and those who have given me support and encouragement.

Client Confidentiality

The profiles included in 'Helping People Change' are mainly composites of clients in order to ensure anonymity. Names in these instances have also been changed to preserve client confidentiality.

Where names are given, the individuals concerned have agreed to share their experiences in this way.

Contents:

Foreword

This book is written chiefly for practitioners, for those who, in one way or another, are helping others make sense of what is happening to them at a time of uncertainty or as the result of unexpected events. The reader may be a counsellor, teacher, nurse, trainer, youth or social worker, someone with a pastoral role - indeed, anyone in a helping role - since change and its effects are what helping is concerned with.

The book is divided into three parts.

The first deals with providing frameworks and an **understanding of aspects of the process of change and transition,** whether the change is willed change or involuntary.

The second examines aspects of **loss, grief and bereavement.**

The third concentrates upon the **helper's role and task** with the intention of providing the reader with an overview of some of the key influences at work in a particular change event, whether it is something which appears straightforward like a job change or something altogether more crisis-laden such as the sudden death of a friend or partner.

In the end, of course, no change is straightforward. It has an impact on **everything** in a person's life, just as it, in turn, is affected by what else is taking place. Indeed, it is the overlapping of effects and influences which create many of the uncertainties and confusions for those experiencing the process of change itself.

When a client says in a time of pained confusion, 'I don't know what's the matter with me; it must be my age or something. I should be able to cope with this better than I am doing. After all I wanted to move house!' then we can be sure there are other influences at work to cause such doubt and unease. It may be there are several other changes being managed simultaneously: the car was broken into last week, a child stayed out all night without saying, a husband's health is clearly in question, no matter what he says ..... Individually, each event is capable of being managed, taken together they add up to overload.

We listeners, on the other side, just never know what else someone is coping with until they tell us, and even then we will not know just how heavy or light the burden of it is - for we all have individual limits in our capacities for coping.

Section I

Change and Transition

'Do not confine your children to your own
learning for they were born in another time.'
Hebrew proverb

'The situation is hopeless - but not serious.'
Hungarian proverb

Chapter One

Change, Development and Transition: The Personal Context

We are constantly challenged to give things up throughout our lives and we may or may not mourn for them. Some things we give up gladly: having to give up going to events we do not like, or giving up a job we hate. These things can be a relief, even a blessing. The more fully we live our lives, however, the less room there will be for any regret over those things we have to give up which we did not care about.

However, if I put off doing things until some time in the future only to find out that the future does not turn out as expected, I may then never have the opportunity to do what was postponed. Through experiences such as this, I will know the extent of the frustration I feel at how I have deprived myself of an experience I could have had, but which I didn't take.

How many of us do this time and again? How many of us plan to do things and never get around to them and then regret the fact that we never did? What a waste! If only we had the courage to act with commitment in the present, which is all we have, then there would be no time for regrets. Of course there would still be mistakes, but they would form the basis of lessons from which we can learn and then move forward.

Spending our lives looking back on all we could have done **'if only...'** and then planning how we would have done it is time wasted twice over. We only ever have the present in which to act, something we all too easily forget.

Social And Personal Change

In many respects, time is a modern invention. Before the Industrial Revolution, life was governed by the rhythms and cycles of nature: the duration of the day, the cycle of the seasons, the pace of the natural world, the speed of the horse. The advent of mechanical processes that operate with indifference to night or day, week in, week out in endless monotony, gave rise to the modern consciousness of time as a commodity to be bought and sold; a rare or precious asset to be measured out and put at a high price.

Our sense of time has changed from the inexorable rhythm of the natural world to something that is within human control and yet paradoxically outside our influence. **We have become victims of that which we created in the belief it would free us.**

Our response to change is then both more heroic, wishing to bring it under our control, and more impotent: we are ever more reminded of our incapacity to direct it, or to influence the pace of what happens to us. Change is bewildering in both its speed and novelty. It is difficult to assess the impact of one set of events before we are thrown into another change. We are in danger of simply accumulating experience at the expense of any significance or meaning.

All this provides a context in which individual lives are lived out, **making the individual biography or 'life cycle' difficult to manage or maintain coherently, causing people to feel increasingly isolated, meaningless and powerless.**

Our social life, our family networks, our social and cultural groupings, our economic alliances and our class system have all begun to break down. Our institutions are collapsing. The transience of human relationships and the lack of permanent stabilising groupings indicate the cost.

Generally, it creates a climate in which traditional sources of support for coping with major changes may well no longer be present in many people's lives. When they are, members of those support systems, friends, neighbours or colleagues are often going through bewildering and complex changes of their own. Often, they too do not know what to make of what is happening to themselves or to us.

Perhaps at no other time in our history have so many people experienced so many changes with so little social and cultural support to help them. We are, in a sense, having to make up our lives as we go along.

The Flight into Conformity

At times of great personal and social upheaval when familiar landmarks are sinking and stable certainties are under question, we are forced to look more closely inside ourselves for answers. This is an unfamiliar and risky process for all too many of us. Instead we look round to see what others are doing in the hope that they will show us that there is one right way to respond. The danger is of a flight into meaningless conformity where everyone is doing what they think is expected, no-one is convinced it is working yet they continue to follow the laid down rules out of fear of standing alone and becoming isolated. Periods of such social conformity are often characterised by empty rituals and pointless social codes in which few believe but which everyone observes.

Support Through Change

In the past, traditions, role expectations, and customs (however limiting and confining) provided individuals with a set of routines, rituals and ways of managing themselves through the predictable crises of social and personal life. This is no longer the case. It is more typical in our present conditions that the phases of a particular change are often unknown to the individual passing through it, making even the predictable crises of life such as adolescence, maturity, mid-life, difficulties in relationships, and marriage breakdowns all appear unpredictable and intrusive.

3

This can make the individual demoralised, taking it as a sign of personal failure, and leaving them with an individual and personal sense of inadequacy for what are universal processes that can happen to any of us.

Knowing that life has identifiable phases and stages can help give reassurance and understanding to individuals travelling through whatever life stage they are passing, when otherwise they might be lost in confusion and difficulty. Rites of passage, initiation ceremonies and rituals to mark out the universal stages of the human journey that have been known in all cultures have now begun to break down in many western societies. **This leaves people isolated inside their experiences, often feeling separated and alienated from those around them.**

It is important to recognise the need to help people be free to feel the way they do. There is a need to recognise that the crises in our lives and the lives of those around us are important challenges that can be welcomed. Indeed they are essential if we are to grow to achieve our full potential.

Change, Development and Transformation

There are, and there will continue to be, enormous changes taking place around us. The pressure for change comes from a wide range of sources; social, political and from the pace of new economic developments. And we should not forget there is also the need for change and growth that comes from within any healthy organism itself as it unfolds in its development. Change is not the same thing as development.

> *Change* is movement from one state to another.
> *Development* is an extension or unfolding of potential.
> *Transformation* incorporates development and includes change.

Change can go in any direction. Change may be predictable or involuntary. It may be a relief or a disappointment. It may bring about positive benefits, or it may lead to regression. Change doesn't have to go anywhere or lead to any result. It may therefore be experienced as an interruption and a discontinuity to an ordered way of living.

Development implies taking hold of a process or managing it, having some degree of understanding and possessing some capacity to influence the direction in which it goes. Development has coherence, pattern. It is an organic unfolding, a bringing forth of what is latent. There is progression into a higher order of operating or experiencing. There may be pain and difficulty attached to the transition but the result of the change is towards higher functioning.

Transformation results in a qualitative shift in state, function and processes involved. A new order of operating comes into play. A new mode of functioning appears. The previous way of operating is not simply replaced but superseded and transcended. The old functions are not necessarily abandoned, but others are introduced that exceed previous limitations. Processes are integrated into a higher order of functioning.

Change and development generate fear and excitement, illusion as well as opportunities, consequences as well as dreams. Inevitably there will be choices to be made.

- **Do we cling to the familiar or can we let go?**

- **Do we sit still and sense the direction to follow, or do we react to whatever force strikes hardest or first?**

- **Can we find the courage to act fully when we know the outcome is always going to be uncertain?**

Frequently, the helper's task is to enable the client to take charge of their point of departure and use it as an opportunity for development and positive growth. It is not the helper's task to tell the individual what they should change and then to take control of that change.

Chapter Two

Working With Aspects of Change

Myths about change

How we understand what is happening to us and those about us strongly influences what we decide we can or cannot do about it. **If we are using inappropriate ideas or have inadequate concepts then the actions which flow from them will not resolve our dilemmas or further our development.** However, having the right answers is of no use if we cannot get people to make use of them. We often hold several ideas about change simultaneously, or move between different ones in rapid succession. They all have appeal at different times but they are all limited in their ability to enable us to move effectively through periods of rapid change, such as the times we are currently experiencing.

Some ideas about the process of change, which most of us hold, are described below:-

Incremental change
Underlying this view is the idea that changes are linear and accumulate in sequence. One change doesn't much affect another until 'the straw that breaks the camel's back' happens - a painful way for anyone to realise that they have been dealing with too much change.

Change as disruption
Change is seen as an interruption to an otherwise predictable order or routine. It is unpleasant and nasty. It ought not to happen and 'If I wait long enough it will go away'

Change as a 'one off'
Change is seen simply as a form of re-organisation. It is viewed as an intrusion to my preferred patterns and routines. But in the end life will turn out to be as predictable in the future as it was in the past.

Momentary change
Once there was a stable state to which we will all one day return. Paradise, as we all know, lies in the past!

Imposed change
External agents impose their ill-considered and unworkable ideas upon what was

once a perfect system. This is another version of longing for a golden era that fades further into the past. It is used as a refusal to grapple with the present.

Change as interruption
Changes are deviations in an ordered and coherent system which is never allowed to operate because of the interruptions. This is akin to the nuisance theory of change ie. change should not take place unless it suits me.

Revolutionary change
The political realities of the situation have changed. Another group is now imposing its will. This leaves us victims once more, unable to contribute anything useful. This is a version of the lie down and die approach to change.

Random change
'No one knows much of anything about any of what is happening so there is really no need to do any more than muddle on as before'.

Programmed change
Change is a blip on the graph of progress that underlies everything that we are doing. 'We are ever nearer the golden future so don't make life difficult. Learn to grin and bear it.'

Change from the outside
In all the views of change stereotyped above, we need to remember that **the maximum potential to have the greatest impact lies in sudden, unpredictable, disruptive, external intervention. This produces alarming confusion rendering the subject open to large scale manipulation which takes a long time to settle. If** this is done repeatedly, both systems and individuals literally have no idea of where they are and therefore have no considered response to offer.
This is something helpers working in organisations undergoing continuous, poorly planned, badly executed change would do well to remember.

Doreen began a counselling relationship to help manage her way through the final stages of leaving her post as a manager in a medium sized organisation. She had felt at odds with the direction in which things were going for some time. Attempts to bring people together to reflect upon the impact of changes within the organisation and how they were affecting staff met with little support. In the end, she decided to seek outside help for herself, evaluate where she stood and what she might want out of the impending changes.

There were other issues in Doreen's life that she knew she could include within a counselling relationship, but she was clear from the outset that the focus of the sessions was to be firmly placed upon enabling her to 'manage her way out.' It would have been too easy, she felt, given what she knew about

herself, to roam all over the 'goings on' in her life and to 'let the job-issue become just one more thing to reflect upon'.

Over the next year we met regularly with the clear contract to look at how she managed her way out of her increasingly difficult situation, as the pressures upon her and her staff mounted. The clarity of her initial commitment enabled Doreen to leave the organisation sufficiently in charge of herself and her future to embark upon a new position with increasing responsibility. Many of her colleagues were astonished at the way she had managed the change and the way in which she had finished her time with the organisation, leaving nothing 'hanging in the air' or left unsaid.

As a final note, many of her recommendations, ironically, are being reconsidered in the light of the difficulties the organisation has encountered following her departure and the lack of success of the changes that were introduced earlier.

Helping someone change, as in this case, may well mean sticking to a clear brief and remaining within a fixed set of concerns, to the client's benefit. Not everyone who looks for help has to unravel the whole of their past life before they can begin to make progress with one specific concern. Sometimes though, it is only by looking at inter-connections that the broader set of inter-playing forces can begin to be seen at work. In such cases, single issues cannot be isolated to be worked with. It needs time to separate out the impact of one issue upon others. Counselling then needs time and opportunity to sift through the concerns and establish priorities about which can be tackled in which order.

Transitions

Transitions are a particular type of change which have within them elements of predictability, growth and development. **There are phases of activity and thresholds which help identify the various stages along the route,** whether this is a transition into a new position at work, a divorce, or the transition into parenthood.

The possibility of learning and integration are important features of all transitions. Much potential learning may be extracted from transitions, providing we understand that there are underlying, predictable and understandable phases and movements contained within them.

Mary came into a counselling relationship because of *the pressure* she was under from work. What this phrase comprised, when we explored it, was the pressure she increasingly felt would come her way from the new, male manager that had recently been appointed. The atmosphere within the section of the organisation in which she worked had always been male-dominated, but now something about the style and the manner of the new arrival left her uneasy. She 'couldn't put her finger on it,' but she was definitely not at ease. A female

colleague had taken sick leave to the point of being retired from post because of similar difficulties. Mary thought there had been more than a lack of interest from the organisation in the well-being of her colleagues. It was, she felt, a way to push people - meaning women - like herself out. She was extremely distressed at this possibility .

Work with Mary took place, meeting regularly, though not frequently, enabling her to clarify the increase in pressure and how far her suspicions about the insecurity of her own post were accurate. Most of the 'female intuitions', that her husband and her manager thought were 'a little far fetched', often proved accurate a little while later. Through these 'hunches', she did see that there was a real change of mood and a new determination to change the working atmosphere in her section and that her own position was being undermined, leaving her with questions about what she might do in the future.

All these work-based concerns however, though central to much of the work between Mary and the counsellor, were nevertheless only a part of a wider story that Mary unfolded to herself as the months went by. Her insecurity and stress reactions were also related to her stage in life and the effects of the menopause. Her family life, though strong and secure, was undergoing change as the last of her children was about to embark upon a University career and leave home. Her husband, an active and involved professional man himself, was facing the prospect of sudden redundancy and the effect this might have upon their future together was a matter of concern. The health of her own parents was also a cause for concern, with Mary having to travel many miles to see them.

As the months of the work went by, Mary was able to recognise that whilst the stress and pressure of the job was all too real and her concerns about her position all too valid, they were related, in part, to a set of wider changes taking place within her life. She was unaware of this before the counselling sessions began. These were the transitions taking place in her own life and those of her family.

The counselling relationship continued whilst Mary worked her way out of her post, taking early retirement to devote more time to ensuring her parents were settled into a new style of accommodation; her husband had left his old job and she had worked out some of the options that she might take up. It was important for her, she maintained, that she sorted out the other people in her life to her satisfaction before she could feel free to concentrate upon what she would do next. 'It gave me a valuable breathing space, those first few months of settling everyone else down, to let me begin to work out what I wanted to do.'

The counselling for Mary was much more about helping her manage her pathway through a set of transitions than it was about helping her to come to terms with a particular change - though the job-change had been the trigger for the entire process and remained the overwhelmingly significant element within it.

The inevitability of change

"No change" is not an option in this life. It is:

"How prepared are we to change?"

"How willingly do we incorporate change?"

"How well can we learn its lessons?"

"How freely can we then move on towards fulfilling our potential?"

Learning to establish oneself in a career, for example, or understanding the difficulties that are involved in moving house - two very common experiences likely to affect everyone between the ages of twenty and thirty - have very predictable phases within them. These phases, once known, can help an individual passing through such changes locate themselves more clearly, enabling them to feel a sense of reassurance that the range and mixture of feelings they experience does not make them odd or strange.

Someone who has looked forward to moving to a new home and who begins to feel depressed within five or six weeks, without knowing why, can be helped enormously when they find out that this is an experience very many people have. Frequently it is the simple aftermath of all the activity of moving and the lack of settled features to the new life.

At a later stage, there may be a return to familiar feelings of depression once again, as there is a recognition of all those things that were left behind in the old neighbourhood. At the time they may have been taken for granted, but now they are sorely missed. They only serve to highlight the lack of routines, new landmarks and new social connections that might replace them.

The Ambivalence of All Transitions

Individuals might get 'stuck' in such changes, unable to understand the sense of failure that stems from what was supposed to have been 'the move of a lifetime.' Of course, it can be that the expectations people have are simply not met in reality and so they have to reassess the future because they were unrealistic in the first place. It may be they desire to sell up and go back to the old neighbourhood, and that might not work either. It simply isn't possible to return to the past and relive it as it used to be. Once you have moved on you have to keep going.

Learning From Change

Such experiences are ones from which all of us can learn. They are all experiences which offer lessons. It may not be possible to guarantee the predictable features of any change, nor that it will turn out as positively as you had hoped. You can only anticipate, consider, review and learn. Planning a change does not guarantee success. It does mean anticipating the likely obstacles and challenges of what lies ahead so that you will be better prepared to face whatever consequences occur.

From Change to Development

Development represents a qualitative change. An event is no longer suffered or endured, but some management and influence is brought to bear upon it which can help to create meaning and provide clues for the direction ahead.

Development is not necessarily gradual or incremental; not a matter of equally sized steps. It can take the form of sudden breakthroughs, jumps and discontinuities and unexpected insights. Development often demands that we work at the thresholds of our understanding; act at the edges of our perception and work closely with the vulnerabilities of our personal identity.

Sandra came into counselling to face the difficulties she was still experiencing following the end of a long term relationship which had been characterised by great difficulty and abruptness. She was a very businesslike woman in her thirties, who had no previous experience of counselling and 'frankly', didn't really know, 'if it would be her thing or not'. She came with a set agenda to 'sort herself out' in a matter of a few weeks, leaving herself free to pick up her busy social life, able once more to be the person everyone always knew her to be - bright, vivacious and successful. She maintained this attractive persona for several weeks and the sessions were indeed of questionable help to her. The whole notion of looking at her own experience, of talking things over with someone else, was alien and 'frankly' (a favourite word) probably 'a waste of time'. But she persisted.

Gradually, she began to recognise that the marvellous relationship she had just lost, was perhaps not quite the romance she had always made it out to be. Perhaps too, the job she had was not altogether so wonderful as she often made it out to be, and maybe her wonderfully attractive and successful social life was not all that it was supposed to be either, but if it wasn't, then what did her life add up to?

Sandra was no longer exploring how to manage a change which had devastated her, but was facing a re-evaluation of the life she had always lived and beginning a fundamental questioning of what it meant. The work from here, if we were to go further, would take on a very different quality to that which had preceded it. No longer were we pretending to make adjustments within a life that was well regulated and satisfying; it was much more a developmental path that she would be treading into the future to create a life quite different from that which she had accepted would be hers.

11

Following her commitment to pursue her own development, Sandra has begun to unravel some of the patterns of her life that link back to her past, her family relationships and the way in which her family life was organised.

A developmental relationship doesn't mean ignoring the past, often it is a return to the past with a new awareness - to find the keys and the clues and the links to help make sense of how the present is influenced by how it was then and to begin thinking of 'How do I want it to be different in the future?'

The Threshold Experience

As we approach a major change, sometimes termed a **threshold experience** we begin to sense our world view being challenged, however mildly, with potential consequences we still cannot foresee. Such moments have with them a sense of inevitability; that however much we might wish to resist what is happening there is another part of us aware that we are simply going to have to go with what is happening. As the Greeks knew, 'He who will, the fates lead and he who won't they drag' There is then a sense that the only choice is whether we go willingly on the journey of the change or whether we struggle and resist the inevitable. There is often a hanging back. Individuals are understandably nervous and cautious of the step ahead and for what it may imply for the future. Such tension creates *ambivalence*. There are often rapid swings of mood from 'Yes I want to change my job,' to 'but what if I don't like the new one?'

Andrew had been exploring the patterns of his life for a good while. He had seen several therapists and counsellors and gained a great deal from each of them. Now, though, things were different. This time something had shifted. Andrew felt 'locked' within a marriage that he was unhappy with and with a partner who was also unhappy. Now there was a new key to open the door to it all. A series of failed attempts to separate, to work things out, to talk together and with other people, attempts to 'talk the relationship into its grave' had all failed. Each of them had tried to begin alternative relationships, in the hope that they would provoke something in themselves, or each other, to bring some change to a very 'stuck' situation. Nothing had worked. They were, of course, trying too hard. So what might bring some change about? The catalyst was a phone call from a colleague from a long time ago, inviting Andrew to become involved in a new project.

There was little convincing evidence that the idea might work. It was outside the scope of his usual assignments and it wasn't an area that appealed to him - or so he thought. 'But you know, it just made everything snap,' he said. 'I realised I could find all the reasons why it made no sense, just like I always do. And I would still be sat here wondering what else to do. It hit me. I could just go and try it and see what happened. After all isn't that what we've spent months talking about - me taking risks? Well, I've agreed and I'm going and I'll work everything out as I go along.'

Two weeks later Andrew was panic stricken at the thought of what he had committed himself to and what the effects would be when it didn't work. Far from being a chance he wanted to test out how to take risks, it had now become a project doomed from the start, simply because he had said he would take part. He hadn't checked the funding arrangements and the more he found out the more anxious he became. His friend was not reliable. He had doubts and hesitations and they grew and grew.

He had got this far before, to the brink, but he had never taken himself over. Was this the time he would? Was this the time I might say just the wrong thing and influence him - one way or another? We both waited, him looking to see if he could get me to decide for him and we both laughed. 'I know,' he said, 'you're not going to decide for me, are you?' 'No', I agreed.

It was enough. He shrugged his shoulders and left. The next time we met he had decided he might as well see it through. He had no great faith in it but....

What Andrew didn't know then, but which stood out a mile from where I was looking, was that he had now crossed over the threshold. It was less important now whether this new step worked or not. In one important respect, it already had. It had provided him with enough impetus to go past that 'hanging in the balance' moment and to see what would happen. He had always drawn back in the past and exercised caution. Now he was willing to live with the risk of having to work things out as they happened. It wasn't the end of Andrew's difficulties, but he was beginning to realise that something he could attempt in one part of his life may apply equally well elsewhere in his life.

In any major change or developmental process there is a stage when the scales tip violently from side to side. At such times we often look to others to tell us what to do in order to relieve ourselves of responsibility for the decision and to put an end to the struggle with all its accompanying anxiety and confusion. This, of course, is a temptation helpers must resist.

This stage of **ambivalence,** as it is termed, is an important aspect of the process of change or development. It is a part of the process of our *coming to terms* and adjusting; of weighing the two sides of the issue. There is, on the one hand, the need to *let go* and give oneself up to the change that is taking place, which many of us find so difficult, and on the other, there are all the hopes and opportunities lying in the future pulling us away from the present and drawing us forward.

Sometimes the ambivalence is about the pain and suffering which lie on either side of the choice we have to make: the pain of staying in a relationship versus the pain of parting. It may take many months, even with help, to reach a decision about something as important as leaving or staying in a relationship, but in such a situation a client must know that they got to their destination themselves, if they are to grow or to develop.

Development and Scripts

Our individual development is linked to our personal biography, or life script. It is a living out of the themes and issues which make up a fundamental part of who we are. Our biography is made up of the combination of issues and difficulties that we struggle with and celebrate. It is linked to our temperament, our inheritance, family background, social class and personal experience. These factors contribute to providing the mixture of experience and conditions which lead us to meet certain issues in our lives and sometimes throughout our lives.

For some time, for example, the theme of health and the struggle to remain well may take up a major portion of our life's journey. At another point it is friendship that produces continuing issues of crisis and development. It might be that work creates a focus for themes to be faced and give rise to pre-occupations over a long period of time. Sometimes there are struggles with dependency issues in relation to drugs or alcohol. In addition there are those other issues that arise at certain stages in an individual's life, no matter what other difficulties they have had to deal with.

These are the **developmental crises** *and they lay the foundations for our future responses.* Satisfactorily completed, a developmental crisis can provide the springboard for a new phase of life and can, in some cases, be of such importance as to initiate a transformation within an individual's life.

David had done what he was supposed to - followed the pattern laid down for him by his father. He had become successful in the way expected. He had married a woman that everyone thought was 'lovely' (his word). He had a successful business. His customers were loyal. They would take him out to lunch, he was so popular. He had a wide circle of friends..... and so the story went on.

David's script was not a grinding, difficult story of pain and struggle. It was rather the reverse; a story of ease and order, of finding it all falling into 'one's lap' and not having very much to do. Looking back over his life, it had always been like that. He had not had to work for anything that mattered. It had all come to him in due course.

Did this matter? It didn't to him. He felt no guilt at what he had. He wasn't unpleasant or unkind toward those less fortunate than himself. He was a concerned member of his local community. It was just that his life, well, it wasn't really his own somehow.

As the work progressed, David began to see more and more clearly how his life script, the pattern of events from the past, laid down a certain set of expectations and situations for things to then unfold in the predictable way they had. His wild ideas, his artistic interests, his imaginative ravings, all these were assigned a place, but not given a recognition of value.

And all might have remained as it was, if it hadn't been for the restlessness of his wife, who was often saying to him that he had become 'boring'. Or maybe

he had always been boring and she was finally noticing it after all these years. He wasn't angry or upset at this criticism, he knew just what she meant because this was a lot like the way he felt about himself.

Working through David's life biography and finding the script patterns that created it was not difficult; changing it was another matter. He knew how to be the way he was; to be any different might mean turning out to be a different person and he was not sure he wanted that.

The sessions took place over some months as David gradually separated out the parts of his past he wanted to value and retain and the parts of his past he wanted to modify in relation to the influence they had upon his life in the present. It is easier to say that than to do it. But David's life is more his own now than it has ever been - something other people are finding out and not always liking - a price David hadn't bargained for when he began changing. 'But at least my wife doesn't say I'm boring any more.'

Transformation

Transformation is a radical shift; a departure from the familiarities of the past; a breakthrough experience. It is a qualitative shift at the level of our being, not simply a growth in understanding or a shift in behaviour. A transformation opens up new ways of responding and experiencing ourselves. It is a move to a new level of functioning that incorporates our previous responses and integrates them into an altogether higher order of functioning. Such changes are manifested on many levels; there will be physical, emotional, intellectual and, very often, spiritual consequences.

Someone living through a transformation may appear physically different. They may well change their wardrobe, friends, ideas, jobs and beliefs. A transformation may be a long time coming (a period of long preparation, albeit unknown to the subject, may be recognisable in retrospect) or begin with a massive upheaval that takes a long time to consolidate.

More Than a Change

However it begins, once established it becomes part of the very structure of the person. They are what they have become. Such experiences do not occur predictably or even with conscious planning. They can only **arrive** at key points in an individual's life, when a door opens beckoning them down a pathway that was almost inconceivable in the past. Possibilities undreamt of suddenly become available and taken. Risks once thought of as being too challenging are taken. It is both exhilarating and frightening. The person undergoing such an experience, and all those around them, can endure much pain and suffering. The determination to follow an impulse that takes over life so strongly can cause fear in others for the safety of the person undergoing the experience, who they see as changing so radically in such a short time.

15

This can give rise to doubts and insecurities about the person's sanity and can lead to many unhelpful responses, including trying to bring the person out of such a change, attempting to stop the process working itself out and trying to influence them to settle down and become *themselves* again. Such anxieties, if *projected* on to the person undergoing the transformation, may well be used as an excuse to contain them and hold them back. Such efforts can create lasting damage and can postpone, or upset, the process of completion.

Trigger Events

A transformation begins by appearing as an accelerated process of change, but it brings with it such a profound level of change that the result is a form of transcendence. A transformation may be triggered by an *unexpected external* event (sudden redundancy or a partner leaving unexpectedly); by a *last straw* experience (the person, usually in retrospect, realises that the trigger event was only the last in a long series); by a *well prepared initiation,* (after long years of meditation there comes a sudden breakthrough), but common to all transformation experiences is:-

- **you cannot make them happen;**
- **you cannot control them;**
- **you do not know where they will lead;**
- **the person concerned is as surprised as anyone else at what happens.**

This makes for a bewildering process. *The similarities between a transformative experience and other emotional and mental disturbances are often strikingly similar.* Not everyone who insults their boss and leaves work is about to undergo a transformative experience, but many people who go through a period in their lives when they are labelled unstable or emotional are living through some version of a transformation experience. More often than not they receive no help or guidance and so do not know the nature of what is happening to them. If they are simply regarded as people *having a breakdown* and treated as such they may well falter in their development risking a setback that can be life-long in its effects.

Tony came to his first session a totally inexperienced client. Yet he spoke with a quiet command, outlined his situation, described the current wave of events that had propelled him in the end to come and find someone to help him sort it out. He was calm and reflective as he spoke and after about forty minutes he paused and said; 'Well, what do you think?'

Here was a man standing at the edge of ruin, a man who was risking his career, his business, his marriage, his circle of friends and his entire assembled life and talking about it with a quiet and a calm that was remarkable.

Why? Because through everything he was doing he was bringing the moment of his exposure more certain and closer, yet he was nevertheless

unrepentant. At the end of the session he said; 'I had hoped that by coming to see someone like you, I would talk about it and it would make me feel better.' 'But it doesn't does it?' I asked. 'It's funny that,' he said, 'you're right. It doesn't.' He was puzzled and I said, 'because you aren't sorry for any of this and you actually quite like it, don't you?' He paused only for a moment, before smiling and saying, 'Yes, I do. I've never felt so alive in my life. I know what I'm doing doesn't make any sense and it's crazy, but I can't stop and I don't want to. For the first time in my life I feel that life itself is unpredictable and I want to see where it leads - even if I live to regret it. I'll always have known that I didn't turn my back on it.'

Judy was already quite a self-aware woman in her late thirties when she first came for counselling. She had been within a routine marriage with a partner that she knew she let hold her back from really taking off. She knew herself to be attractive, capable and relatively ambitious. So, 'Why,' she was asking herself, had she 'stayed in a relationship which clearly held me back?' There had to be some pay off for all this.

But what had really brought her to seek time and space to sort out her future was the decision she had already taken to leave her marriage. It had been provoked by her meeting someone else. But, she was clear, the someone else was only the catalyst for her to do something she 'should have done years ago' and whether this relationship worked out or not was not really her concern: yet it had been important enough to begin the process of change she so needed.

Within the space of three sessions Judy had transformed her wardrobe, changed her address, her diet and her life style. She was living alone, spending time by herself and working out what she wanted for herself in a way that she had never previously attempted. Suddenly, she was aware of just how limiting she had allowed her marriage to make her. Another session later and she was already planning a new career move, since she realised that she overworked, needed less money than she was presently earning and had long-standing ambitions to fulfil that she had never given herself the freedom to seek.

There is more work to do to enable Judy to find out how all these things are linked to the settling for a marriage which she used to keep her from fulfilling herself. She may or may not do that work, but what is clear is that she has passed through a transformative experience and she will never go back to the accommodating woman she once knew herself to be.

Chapter Three

Influences Upon Personal Change

Ambivalence Towards Change

Any desire we might have to embrace change has to overcome our desires and impulses to keep things the way they are or to restore the past. This is a universal feature of the human response to the process of change. **Resistance to change** is an important dimension to any work with change and yet the fact remains that despite all the resistance we may mobilise towards some changes or to aspects of some changes, *human beings are marvellously adaptable.*

Learning to Adapt to Change

The ability to learn from experience relies on the stability of the interpretations we use to predict the pattern of events. We assimilate new experiences by organising them within the context of a familiar, reliable construction of reality. This mental structure in turn rests not only on the regularity of events, but on the continuity of their meaning what we are used to them meaning. When we offer our hand in friendship we do not expect to be struck with a blow across the face!

In this way, we impose regularity and order upon events which are not always exactly alike, nor are they always regular. But we learn how to disallow those features within experiences which are unique or novel in favour of those which conform to the meaning we both expect from the situation and bring to it.

We all know what *lighting up* time is and we all know it varies from day to day. We all know what the *tide* is and we all know tides change. We are willing, in such examples, to look for and establish the underlying law or pattern which regulates such events. In the case of lighting up time these laws and patterns will vary according to social customs, time and place whilst changing tides will vary according to the laws of nature.

We would not be able to survive without some system, or a series of systems that enable us to predict and ascribe meaning to events and in one sense the explanations that we follow do not have to be right or true in any absolute sense, only **useful** and **agreed** by those observing them. They have to provide guaranteed results not right ones.

Marris points out that:

'The predictability of behaviour is profoundly important, and it depends not

only on some shared sense of the meaning of relationships but on conventions of expressing this meaning which, must be insisted on all the more anxiously because they are arbitrary.' (P.7)

Our social life is constructed according to the rules of social convention and without them we would be plunged into meaninglessness. Many people become highly threatened at the least challenge to the status quo because it threatens to reveal that **the social world is held together by a very fragile sense of agreement.**

From the Social to the Personal

Just as in social customs, so too **in a personal way, we consolidate experience into consistency in order to assemble the assumptions that shape our life and predict for us the meaning of what will happen, what is happening and what has happened.**

This is an important form of learning from experience and is crucially linked to our early attachment experiences and sense of security. The assimilation of new experience depends upon us possessing pre-existing organising structures able to incorporate it. As long as the modifications and changes demanded of us by new experience remain tolerable then we can find a way of accommodating to the consequences within the limits of consistency and continuity.

We all feel threatened if our basic assumptions and emotional attachments are challenged because they in turn challenge the regularity of the predictable world we pretend we live in.

Over time, the action and purposes we give ourselves, which in theory could find expression of satisfaction in any number of ways, become associated and shaped to particular relationships, the setting or the individual involved. We cannot be separated from them without a threat of anxiety resulting.

As a result of this process, meaning derives from the consequences or the results we attach to what we do. **We attribute significance to events according to their expected outcomes in relation to our pre-established mental and emotional categories and this in turn guides our response to them.**

This helps explain why it may take many, many sessions and much agonising for someone to free themselves from a job or a relationship, which they *know* to be ultimately undermining them or doing them no good. The underlying pattern of consistency and the ability of the job or the relationship to have found a fit with the person's world of events and experience means it is not simply a case of changing it and it alone but of the knock on effects the one change will have upon the rest of the person's life.

Jane was very clear that there was much in her relationship that she would like to change. She knew she wanted her partner to be more involved with the children and to take an increasing role with domestic aspects of life. She

19

thought of her partner as another child who would now have to grow up, because there were twins suddenly to look after! The shock of two children when only one was expected had led June to re-evaluate her relationship and what she wanted. But very soon she realised the changes she was seeking were not likely to come about from the man she married. She began to face the fact that if she placed the kinds of pressure upon him that would be needed to get him to change, the relationship would not stand the strain. 'And I want my marriage to work more than I need to make us all unhappy to see him change, because I know he just won't be able to do it.' How far she was right or not; how far she should have campaigned for her rights as mother or a woman were not the issues for her counselling session. She had come to clarify the impact of having two children that she had not expected and to find out what adjustments could be made to the marriage as she knew it. *She came to her own conclusions.*

Modifying Our Views

Of course new events do modify our existing frames of reference;

'Experience influences purpose, purposes influence the relevance of experience, both become integrated in more or less comprehensive structures, where specific expectations and desires are subsumed under general principles of action. But as we grow up the structures become more and more difficult to revise, by virtue of their very success.' (Marris P.10)

Over time we stabilise the internal meanings and contexts by excluding differences and since our ability to cope depends upon our sense-making capacity anything which threatens our conceptual structures, our beliefs and assumptions, we find profoundly disturbing. The more fundamentally challenged we are, the more crucially we find ourselves having to revise the very structures of belief themselves. I begin by having no doubts about a particular action of my partner: but then I reach a point where I doubt their essential honesty.

The Influence of Context

The context in which an event takes place is less open to revision than the events themselves. Meaning is acquired in context and is context-related. As a result, we may not know how to translate our learning from one context to another where it may be as useful, or more useful, nor do we know how to stop behaving in some contexts with behaviours which apply to others that may seem similar.

Much social comedy is based on these kind of discrepancies. Someone is placed in a situation with inadequate understanding of the context and the resulting mis-match creates embarrassment and mayhem all round.

Many people, for example, can be assertive at work but not at home. Some people can act decisively in their leisure time pursuits, hang-gliding or water-skiing, for example, but vacillate in their personal lives.

Survival

One consequence of the need for a consistency of our attachments and meaning may well be that those who hold their principles of life to be absolute, universal and unchallengeable may survive in a situation of extreme uncertainty, where the more open-minded may be destroyed by their inability to derive any intelligible regularity from events around them.

Continuity of Purpose Versus Novelty of Experience

We need confidence in the continuity of purpose and the sense of regularity in our social behaviour or we begin to lose the ability to interpret the meaning of events. The threat of chaos is never far away. Yet we must at the same time remain open to the revision of our purposes and understandings or we lay ourselves open to making disastrous mistakes.

Then we meet the greatest of all challenges. How do we know at what point we should change our assumptions? How do we know when we have? How do we know when we weren't fooling ourselves? All of us have had the experience of having changed our minds only to find our mind changed back! We may often change our view but not the underlying structure of belief upon which the view is founded.

Following this process of accommodation, modification, rejection, and revision within limits, we may sometimes encounter events which so contradict or invalidate crucially important assumptions which structure the meaning of what happens to us that we become threatened by psychological disintegration. *In such circumstances the very process of our sense-making itself is challenged.*

'Once he admitted that he was having the affair after he had spent all those months denying it, well, that was it. I knew I'd never trust him again. No matter what he said. I'd always be wondering; "Oh yes, and what else is there you are not telling me?"' Unfaithfulness was hard for Elizabeth to face and difficult to come to terms with, but what brought her to the decision to bring the relationship to a close was the importance she attached to truthfulness and not being lied to. She found that a surprising discovery, because she always thought it would have been the affair and the feeling of rejection and deceit that it caused, that would have driven her to leave the marriage. But to her surprise, she found herself able to cope with that once it had happened. It was the lack of trust in the future truthfulness of her partner that meant she was unable to remain in the marriage.

Objective Knowledge and Social Understanding

Systems of knowledge, subject matter or ideas, are much easier to assimilate because we look upon them as self-contained limited structures which we can regard with relative detachment - unless we become heavily invested in them, in which case we can defend our ideas as strongly as our person.

Social understanding is quite different because the underlying connections of elements to one another and how they relate to the broader meanings of our total experience differ from purely personal knowledge.

The more personal knowledge is thrown into doubt, the more painfully difficult action becomes because individual understanding and our personal views, sometimes known as our **'frame of reference'**, is such an idiosyncratic construct. The process of sustaining meaning is so much more an active task than absorbing received ideas - however strongly they may be presented or offered in terms of being for our own good.

This is something that those who are hoping to persuade others into changing rarely understand sufficiently. It is not the information alone that brings about change - most smokers have all the information they need to be terrified at what might lie in wait, but it doesn't stop them smoking.

Change and Regression

We should not forget either that a great deal of change is the result of the process of biological unfolding and that a good deal of other changes which take place in our lives are the result of choice and innovation. In such change, and indeed in change which is externally imposed or enforced by constraints over which we have no control, there is likely to be periods of **regression.**

Regression plays an important part in the overall process of change and growth. It can be viewed as a form of withdrawal or retreat to recover energy for renewed effort. Adolescence and mid-life are both life stages in which periodic regression is to be expected.

Change may also be eagerly anticipated and complaints of boredom (in children especially) often indicate a lack of sufficient (age appropriate) challenge.

Bill had stayed in the same job for ten years - he was always about to leave; he was always looking for something else. Just at the point when he might do something, he was always offered a new post, or new duties, or a chance to do something that he hadn't done before. And then later, he would be on the point of leaving again. He knew the circle. He travelled around it well and soon so did I. Did he intend ever to change, or was he simply going to rehearse the potential for change again and again? Changing jobs was like an old friend, it gave him something to talk about and plenty to think about.

Maybe he got bored with it, or maybe things changed, but whatever it was, when he arrived to say he had not only applied for, but actually got, another job,

both of us were surprised. What finally made it now rather than then? At first, Bill couldn't work it out. But what he realised was that all the rehearsal was important and only now was he ready. At any other stage he would not have been able to leave and take up another post with the degree of confidence he now had. Rehearsals and regression had been an important means of preparation, even though it often did not feel like it at the time.

Change and Growth

The overall process of maturation is not especially disruptive. As long as the thread of continuity is maintained, the anxiety of change can be managed and the more successful the child is in adjusting, the longer the periods of exploration away from the security of the parent figure become.

Similarly, the self-confidence of maturity is not a rejection of support, but an ability to turn for reassurance when the need arises trusting that it will, in all likelihood, be met. But if basic needs have been unmet or if they were erratically or unpredictably satisfied, growing up can all too easily become a succession of bereavements, broken dreams and incomplete attachments.

Confident exploration arises out of the regularity and consistency of the satisfaction of basic needs - security, love and recognition - that allows for later building upon well established patterns of trusted expectations. Such a base creates the opportunity to seek out new skills, experiences and abilities and only the limits of maturation then determine future possibilities.

Angela was a concerned parent, so much so she attempted to live out all the potential scenarios of all her children, just to make sure that whatever they might do they would be safe. If, in her scenario, there was any risk, she felt obliged to point it out to the child and make sure they did everything to avoid that particular risk from happening. The idea that by doing this she might be trying to live their lives for them, or attempting to control them, was at first quite unbelievable. After all, a responsible parent doesn't want their child to have to undergo dangerous or unpleasant experiences which could be avoided with a bit of mature forethought from a concerned parent. 'Wasn't that what parents were for?' Angela had a lot of beliefs about how far a parent should intervene in a child's life - even when she saw it not only did no good, but actually provoked her children into doing the very things she was warning them against. She hadn't realised how precisely she instructed them in ways of doing things that would worry and annoy her. And she didn't like the implications when she discovered this. If all her good advice was not always taken and she really did not have the influence she felt was so necessary; not only was she a bad parent, but her children were at risk from all manner of social dangers.

It took Angela some time to realise that she had done a 'good enough' job parenting all her children, since the things they did that she didn't like fell a

23

long way short of either criminal activities or dangerous social behaviour. She needed to 'let go'. They were all teenagers and needing to explore their own boundaries; able to come back to her and her husband, if needing to talk things over. And when she thought about it, she realised that only she carried this burden, her husband didn't. And perhaps this was not because he cared any the less, but because he trusted the children the more and they knew he was there for them if needed. Whereas she knew that whenever they wanted help from her, she would usually deliver a lecture first, before showing the real underlying concern she had for them.

It took some time for Angela to find a new way to parent her growing children, but she did it.

The Balance Between Continuity, Growth and Loss

We can distinguish different kinds of change in terms of the balance between continuity, growth and loss.

Incremental changes (or substitutional changes) leave the individual's overall sense of expectation and purpose essentially unaffected. A new car, for example, is an alternative means of meeting a familiar need (this is a case of substitutional change). The overall continuity of life remains largely unaffected. However a gathering number of such incremental changes may accumulate to create a crisis - a house move disrupts the continuity of life at many levels and in major ways, creating significant losses for which there are no immediate remedies.

When change takes the form of **growth,** the individual's sense of overall purposes and expectations are not disrupted but incorporated within a greater range. Such changes may represent a great step to the individual without threatening what has been learned from the past. Indeed, it may represent a demonstration of the success of past learning - the move into a new position of increased responsibility for example.

Such a step can only be accomplished on the foundation of the internal security achieved from past experience. In time of course, and with hindsight, this very step may come to be seen with a measure of naivety in the light of future experience. But at the time the step itself was taken it is nevertheless a demonstration of extending beyond past achievements.

Change may represent **loss,** either foreseen or unforeseen. This may vary all the way from death itself, or the loss that may result from the breakdown of assumptions - finding a lack of trust in a friend for example. In such circumstances the loss is experienced as a change that takes the form of an unexpected discontinuity and this results in despair and disillusionment however briefly and, if serious enough, our familiar ways of interpreting our experience become suspended altogether.

The more fundamental the challenge, the more distress will follow and yet if life is to go on our continuity has to be restored. When loss is irretrievable only a re-interpretation that is both radical and yet plausible can recreate the necessary sense of continuity that we all require if we are to go on.

This involves accepting the loss as an experience which requires us to engage in the process of understanding and not simply view it as an event, as something which happened. We also have a need to review the overall context in which the event took place.

Redundancy hit Walter with all the force of a blow. He often described the effect as being 'pole-axed'. Though it was not altogether unexpected, he was not prepared for it or for its effects. He was not someone who had read a great deal and since the same experience was happening to many in his community, he found little help anywhere. His mates were all making a pretence of managing, but he knew that underneath most of them, like himself, were unable to manage or cope with the devastation and the loss. A job had not simply gone; what he was mourning was the passing of a way of life. And though mining was difficult and dangerous work, it did create a sense of belonging and connection between families that was already slipping away.

The work for Walter was long and difficult. For the first time in his life he had to face being alone, with no sense of a group of people standing around him, being with him. The sense of solidarity that existed in his mining community was not something he could draw upon when facing the loneliness and pain of having no work to do and the feeling of emptiness and purposelessness that this brought about.

As much as coming to terms with redundancy, Walter had to find and then meet himself in a way that neither his background nor his education had prepared him for. It was a long time before any new step forward was possible for him.

The Importance of Both Purpose and Meaning

The nature of the response we make to any change turns upon the relationship between these crucial forces: the continuity of purpose and the continuity of broader meaning. Change, experienced as a novelty, is more easily incorporated into our usual pattern because we are more able to reduce it to some form of substitution or improvement. Change as growth comes out of our imposing new purposes on the circumstances we face and whose meaning has not been disrupted.

'Bereavement follows from the disintegration of a meaningful environment without any change of purpose - though out of bereavement a new sense of purpose may emerge in time.' (Marris P.22)

Chapter Four

The Change Process

An individual's overall life circumstances at the time of entering a particular change or transition will markedly affect their response. There are two aspects to the phrase life circumstances.

1.   External Aspects of Life

Within this category falls such influences as: *the network of relationships, our surroundings and the environment; paradigm shifts; the quality of relationships; the variation in incident and activity and levels of satisfaction.* These external factors will have a sharp influence and are relatively easy to identify.

Paradigms of Understanding

'Paradigm' comes from the Greek word meaning pattern. A paradigm of understanding is a given framework of thought, a way of explaining certain aspects of reality. The Theory of Gravity, for example, offers a paradigm which helps explain the laws of the physical world. Paradigms explain the way things are and cover every field of human activity and understanding. They are the belief systems and assumptions that govern the way we look at an aspect of life.

Paradigms seem total and complete explanations that will last for ever because they are the dominant and agreed way of describing things, but from time to time a paradigm comes under increasing pressure and if the pressure is strong enough the paradigm may have to be given up altogether in favour of a new description. In our present time we can see the paradigms of explanation doing just that in one field after another.

We are living through a period of paradigm shifts in politics (the collapse of communism); economics (the return of the recession that was never supposed to happen and is already over, yet somehow mysteriously remains); in culture (the breakdown of the liberal consensus) and we are searching around for new ways to understand and explain our situation to ourselves. The failure of our long established explanations to make sense of the rapid social and political changes at work across the world have contributed to the underlying sense of social upheaval and disturbance. This creates a context of such great uncertainty for individuals to work out their own choices about life and destiny that would be hard to exaggerate.

In addition, individuals arrive at moments of such serious challenge that their previous world view and fundamental assumptions have to give way. At an individual level, we may well experience something akin to a paradigm shift.

When new data no longer fits the existing framework we are presented with a problem: either we discount the new data and maintain the theory's validity, or we find ways to incorporate the incongruities within it. For example we might claim that 'this was an exceptional experiment so it doesn't count', but the new information keeps piling up, the anomalies increase and the contradictions become more obvious. In the end there is so much new information which cannot find a place in the old paradigm that a crisis ensues. This is essentially a crisis of belief.

At this stage someone usually comes along and proposes what seems like a wacky or heretical explanation. Some outlandish insight is put forward to explain the contradictions. This includes a new principle or a new perspective.

New Paradigms

The new paradigm, or theory, for that is what it is, is more inclusive and comprehensive than previous explanations and therefore represents progress and development. A new paradigm is a hierarchical improvement. Usually the old paradigm is not abandoned altogether, it is retained as a useful framework for those activities to which it remains relevant.

Newtonian physics, for example, is still useful and valid for explaining some phenomena but not all. Einstein's Special Theory of Relativity superseded the Newtonian paradigm. The theory of relativity provided an alternative explanation that could incorporate a great many of the anomalies that didn't fit in with the Newtonian view.

In simple terms, Einstein provided a convincing explanation to show that Newton's work which established causal chains of cause and effect, essentially a mechanical view of the Universe, did not apply to vast bodies such as galaxies nor infinitely small particles such as electrons. Within its range of applicability, the Newtonian paradigm works; it simply did not anticipate being superseded because phenomena outside its range would one day be discovered.

The Implications of a Relative Universe

The revolution that this brought to our thinking is only just beginning to enter into the field of Communications and Counselling. 'It takes fifty years,' one scientist said, 'before a scientific discovery penetrates the public.'

A new paradigm reveals a principle that was always present, but simply not apparent. It includes the previous explanation as a partial rather than whole truth. The introduction of a new, larger perspective brings about new questions to explore, as well as predicting solutions to problems with more accuracy. In short, it is a better explanation of what we know as well as a spur and a stimulus to find out more about what we don't know.

Resistance to New Ways

Surprisingly, given its value and its release of potential, a new paradigm does not take hold easily or immediately, and this is largely because you can't take on a new paradigm without admitting the old one is inadequate and letting it go. You can't do it piecemeal; it has to be taken on board as a whole.

New paradigms are generally greeted with resistance and even hostility; Copernicus, Galileo, Pasteur, Mesmer, were all subject to attack for proposing their new ideas. New ideas are seen as bizarre or 'wacky', and whilst they are still in their infancy and are new and undeveloped they are easy to attack.

Gaining Acceptance of a New View

New paradigms gain ascendance as new thinkers enter the field uncluttered by previous assumptions. When their numbers reach a critical mass the shift occurs and the field as a whole embraces the new view of things. But it too, in turn, becomes another orthodoxy waiting to be undermined.

Part of the problem of paradigm shifts is that they are very much more erratic and irregular than most descriptions of them usually manage to convey. Most descriptions make them appear as though they are a slow and inevitable process rather than a bitterly contested, eruptive, transformative leap, fought out fiercely by those people who have a stake in the final outcome. In our own day, for example, there is a major dispute about the influence of Robert Gallo on the development of research into the HIV virus.

One way to sense a paradigm shift is when the solution offered to the problem doesn't work and hasn't for a while; it is simply a demand for more of the same. More horses and more men didn't actually put Humpty Dumpty together again!

In both social and personal terms the times we live in are making old ideas out of date and new ones difficult to choose between. How do we know which ideas would better suit us when we don't know what kind of world we are going to have to live in? If this is a feeling you have had, you are in the process of adjusting some of your basic beliefs; a paradigm shift.

2.   Internal Aspects of Life

The second group of influences are much more personalised and come from within the individual. They include a *person's self-image, sense of values and expectations of themselves*. They include a lot of intangible and barely thought out ideas about *the individual's inner world*. It is this which is almost impossible to assess, but which will have most impact on how the mover responds to change. We can refer to these internal circumstances as their **frame of reference.**

Frame of Reference

A person's frame of reference is, by definition, unique. You cannot assume that you know what it is. You have to check repeatedly to ensure that you have some understanding of its make-up. **This means the same event will have a variable impact according to how it is understood by those experiencing it.** It also helps explain why individual coping styles vary.

Not only is an individual's frame of reference unique, and therefore unknowable, it is often hidden even from themselves. We often do not really know what we value in a situation or in an experience until we are challenged to compare it, choose or decide about it for some reason.

Lynda was describing the man in her life. With great affection and warmth she described his charming haphazard sense of time, his unpredictable patterns of behaviour and his very individual way of showing his own love and affection. Whilst this was in part maddening, it was also very pleasurable to Lynda. However, the more she talked the more she realised that a life with this man would bring her up against her own view of herself. 'I've always thought of myself as a feminist, but if I live with him I can see it will be my career that will go and it will be his work and his life style that will dictate what we do much of the time'. Lynda's conscious frame of reference about the importance of her feminist values in her frame of reference was under challenge. Did the relationship as she knew it would be, mean more to her than holding on to the definition of herself that she had prized for a long time?

At such times we are often confronted with a decision or a choice that requires us to make conscious the importance of different elements in our frame of reference. The choice we might make may not be the one we would either expect or, in some ways, want.

Whether or not an individual has any available attention to give to the crisis they are in will also affect their response. A person living at a high level of stress will have no 'slack in the system' to respond to yet another demand. How far an individual has an area of their life free from the effects of the transition they are undergoing will influence how well they respond. Stable friendships at a time of changing career can give great reassurance. Familiar routines at work can help a person as they go through the trauma of a broken relationship.

Developmental Stage

The age and phase of life the individual is passing through presents characteristic challenges and predictable crises. Establishing an independent life, for example, usually occurs in our society between the ages of eighteen and twenty-five.

The loss of a parent to a young person will have different consequences to the bereavement of a son or daughter in mid-life. The age and stage we are moving

29

through, and how successfully we have met the challenges of the past, will have an influence on how we cope now.

Cultural, Social, Role and Personal Expectations

The culture we belong to, the social group we live within, and the roles we play all provide ready-made expectations of how we are supposed to respond. We also 'internalise' these expectations until they become our own. These expectations can severely limit a person's freedom to feel the full extent of the emotions and problems relating to the events they are living through, often with unhealthy results. They can shape behaviour and responses to such a degree that the individual repeatedly recreates the same situation in a futile attempt to overcome the problem. Some people move from job to job like nomads, in the belief that it will all work out at the next place. Some of us do the same with our relationships.

The Nature and Type of Change and Transition

Some events are inherently more difficult to face than others. Losing your car keys is obviously not as agonising as losing a child. Facing death is more severe than facing an insensitive critic. However, it must be remembered that it is not always true that we can tell how seriously others will rate a particular experience, because we do not have their frame of reference. Predictions of how much others are suffering are very hard to make and are often unreliable.

Intensity of the Event

How intensely an event is experienced will influence its effect. The sudden and unexpected news that someone close to us has had a fatal accident is usually more difficult to respond to than the death of someone after a prolonged illness.

Duration and Frequency

How long the event lasts, and how often it occurs, has to be taken into account. Short, sharp shocks may be as debilitating as prolonged, low-grade and repeated uncertainty over which the individual has little control.

Relationship to Other Events

How many other changes is the person coping with? Is this particular event one of a series? A large number of small changes that are not being managed well may have a telling cumulative effect, every bit as serious as a major crisis. Such a series of changes may be harder to deal with because there is no single obvious reason for the reaction when someone finally gives up under the accumulated pressure of struggling with prolonged chronic levels of stress.

Chapter Five

Mental Maps

Changes and Beliefs

Whenever we are presented with a challenging situation we depend upon our pre-programmed responses and beliefs to ensure that the significance of what is happening is made to fit in with our current view of the world. It is only natural that we think about and describe any change in ways which make it easier for us to live with. We want the change to adapt, to fit in with our categories and systems of thought and we are often more willing to change our experience of what is happening than change our response. When faced with the discomfort which may accompany a change, most of us would rather change our experience and re-define it so that we are able to believe that we remain in control.

Changing our beliefs in the light of new experience is a risky business and there is no knowing where it might lead. Many people, for example, have had the experience of losing some common-place object and looking around the home for it; sometimes two or three times. As they go from place to place, they look again and again just where they know the object isn't, even saying to themselves such things as, 'I know it's not there'. It is as though we are somehow reassured to know that things aren't where they aren't and simultaneously hoping that they are and we have simply overlooked them. We may not know where they are but we do know where they aren't! And who knows, they might turn out to be there if we just go back and look again! This is a small illustration of our attempt to make the world fit in with our wishes.

A more important aspect of the power of our beliefs over our experience is illustrated in the following story.

A friend of mine was travelling by cycle in Ireland. He had planned a coastal ride for his last day. By mid-morning he was becoming more and more troubled by the mountains in front of him; they were not on the map! For a period he was in a state of uncertainty.

The map said one thing, his eyes told him quite another and he did not know which to believe. Answer? They were both right! True, there were no mountains on the map, but the mountains were there. Foreshortening, and the optical effects of sunlight on water had made the distant Scottish mainland look so close as to be ahead of him!

How often do we approach major changes in just this way? We know what's supposed to be expected so we ensure that it happens and if it doesn't happen the way it is supposed to then we invent it, just as we learned to invent the results of our science experiments at school when they didn't fit the answers we were supposed to get.

Once we have made our experience fit our beliefs and expectations, we overlook everything which doesn't match. Such **selective perception,** as it is known, reinforces our belief system and our world view. We develop elaborate ways of deluding ourselves by distorting experience in this way so that we remain convinced of whatever we wish to be the case. We can always find evidence to support anything we want to believe. Another way of saying this is that we are all good at pretending.

Boundaries and Limits

Each of us lives in our own inner world, a world which is self created and self sustaining. In many important ways we make our own reality out of what happens around us by selecting out what to notice and in deciding the meaning events and experiences will hold. Red light means 'Stop', simple. But what does that look on his face really mean? Meaning, as we all know, is not always simple and straightforward to establish, especially in human relationships and yet, if we did not make assumptions, life, social life especially, would become impossible.

Hence the dilemma: if I make assumptions I will sometimes make mistakes, but I won't know that until I have made them. This is part of the way we learn and we all know that it is not easy. Experiences throughout life help us acquire a largely unconscious sense of identity and a set of boundaries that we rely upon to protect it. We can be every bit as protective about our possessions and ideas as we can about our person. Our personal boundaries help us know who we are, where we end and others begin and whether we feel safe or not.

We also have limits and limitations; thresholds that we will not go beyond without a great deal of support and a sense of safety. Some of our limits are physical. We cannot fly. Some are psychological and seem every bit as true as the statement that 'I cannot fly', but they are nevertheless simply personal limits. 'I'm no good at tennis' for example, or 'I'm hopeless with children.' These kinds of limitations are extremely powerful in their influence upon our conduct. They are usually unchallengeable and entirely self fulfilling. Whenever their absurdity or irrationality is pointed out, we will usually have a convincing rationalisation to explain away anything that is uncomfortably at odds with our view of ourselves. If all else fails we can always rely upon the notion that a contrasting example is simply the exception that proves the rule. Such self-imposed limits ensure that we don't change however much we say we would like to.

Underneath such self-defeating limitations is sometimes a sense of **helplessness**; 'I don't know how to do it' or, what's worse, **hopelessness**; 'I couldn't do it, so I don't need to think about it' or worst of all, a sense of worthlessness; 'I'm not valuable enough to even consider this and I would only fail if I tried.'

Such powerful beliefs often exist at the level of bodily sensations rather than being stated in words. They may not even have words to them, just a certain feeling of powerlessness at the very thought of attempting whatever might be suggested. Sometimes they are accompanied by re-runs of old 'messages' given to us by parents, other adults, or peers who have made fun of our clumsy efforts in the past, often at school. The consequence is that we are left feeling bad enough each time we approach a similar situation that we give up all further effort.

Challenging such self-limiting beliefs is not easy because they link very strongly to our self-image and our sense of identity.

Approaching Thresholds

As we face change, or consider a new course of action, our boundaries and limits are likely to surface. The assumptions we hold will begin to become conscious. It may take some time to unravel how these assumptions operate before we are prepared to consider challenging them by experiment. This process we can term a **'threshold experience'**.

As we move closer and closer to the point of change and feel events gathering momentum, we are likely to experience a sense of uncertainty and sometimes fear inside ourselves that is out of all proportion to the size of the event itself. We know we will survive. We know it is really not that serious an event, and yet it feels so awful that it is as though our very survival is at stake. The nearer we get to a threshold, the more strongly this sensation grows.

This is a strong indicator of a boundary or limit coming under threat of challenge. Such feelings are usually associated with the fear of losing control, or even of going 'out of control'. The sensations may become so acute that we are literally paralysed for a time, before the momentum of the situation gathers and becomes strong enough for us to break through. Once the break-through occurs we may then become overwhelmed by the pace of change and the need to respond.

It is as though the energy locked into holding the change process back is suddenly released with the acceptance, or the decision to go with the change. The result is a helter-skelter feeling of trying to catch up with oneself. This can be exhilarating as well as disturbing and can become addictive.

In her present job, Betty felt squeezed. She knew what she wanted to do, but didn't really think she was capable. (The fact was, she was already doing it, albeit surreptitiously and with no recognition, either by herself or by her employers.) She had gradually found herself more and more at odds with herself and her role, in conflict with the work she did and the needs of the situation in which she was supposed to act. The tensions between what she increasingly recognised was needed and what was offered were getting more and more of a strain to manage. Meanwhile the part of her work that she did like most and found greatest satisfaction in - talking to people about the

33

difficulties she was supposed to sort out - she was finding more and more absorbing even though her workplace needed her to get results. She was caught in a double bind.

The more she worked the more she found herself drawn to what was least legitimate in her role. The more she looked at what was needed, the more alienated she was becoming with her agency. How long could it go on? 'Oh, indefinitely', she thought. 'Until what has to happen?' I asked. She guessed it would go on until she got herself caught in a dilemma that would mean her being disciplined for failure to stay within the limits of the agency's work, or for responding in ways that she felt were needed, but which were at odds with the agency's policy.

The threshold experience. She knew what she wanted and she knew equally well that she couldn't have it. Yet she knew she couldn't go on as she was either, without something serious occurring.

And she had some beautiful excuses as to why she could do nothing to change things. She needed money - as though what she was wanting to do would pay her nothing. She needed the security of a steady job and how secure is the one she had? Less and less so, and possibly not at all. Certainly no more secure than what she wanted to do. And so it went on. The time went by; the crisis became more acute and she was being pushed ever nearer the limit where she would have to decide. What kept it at bay was her ability always to find *'either or'* choices. 'If I do what I want and it didn't work out, then what about..?' 'How would I manage for money if...?' The choices were always constructed as opposing polarities.

She would not see the potential for drawing out of the present those things that would help her move nearer to where she wanted to be and which would enable her to test out the feasibility of what she really wanted to do. And when she was confronted with the fact that she was already doing the thing she most loved - talking to people - and all she had to do was to begin taking more responsibility for it and find ways to get the training she needed to do it etc, she knew she couldn't stay on the far side of the threshold any longer. She was on her way. And she is well on her way.

Control

Control is a major issue for all of us. 'Who is in control?' 'Am I in control?' 'Control yourself!' Control is a big word. We pride ourselves on having control. We look upon others who have not got it as being somehow deficient. But in many important respects we cannot ever control ourselves. We can, however, manage ourselves. We cannot control others either; we can influence them.

The control issue is made so much worse for many of us because we have the illusion that we 'should' be in control at all times and that releasing feelings or expressing emotions are signs of weakness. The effort we then expend to 'stay in control' is often counter-productive. What we are trying so desperately to withhold gathers force and finds expression in other situations, or leaks out inappropriately.

Why do we have such a need for control? Because we need to feel in charge of our own world, because we then feel safe, or so we believe. We need to feel that we are in control, even if we know we are not. The need to struggle to keep control is very strong and people go to enormous lengths to hang on to the illusion that they have it.

When we approach a threshold our need to stay in control gets stronger as our efforts to sustain it become more and more questionable. We look to anyone and anything to *make it better,* to take away the pain, or the prospect of it.

If we are unfortunate someone does appear who attempts to do just that; leaving us drained and frustrated, because in our heart of hearts we know that at some later stage we will have to go beyond the point we have just reached. If someone allows us to get off the hook at this stage, it only means we will be left to find another occasion to learn the lesson that we missed. The journey has to begin once more.

If, however, we are more fortunate and instead meet someone who will enable us to stay *in it;* someone who can hold us safely and enable us to experience the gathering sense of awfulness and fear, the sense of insecurity and helplessness which so often confronts us when we face a challenge from inside ourselves, or from the world outside; someone who can give that sense of being able to hold us that allows us the time to collapse and give way, to feel what is happening before moving on, then we may experience change in a dramatically different way.

This may well then be followed by a whirl-wind rush of energy as the threshold gives way.

At this point we still remain in need of the care and attention of a skilled helper to keep us in contact with ourselves. Such a new sense of freedom can be as addictive as any drug and we can indeed believe that we can do the equivalent of flying. For a time, all sense of proportion may desert us altogether. After all, we have left our old selves behind and our old fears with it. What we feared so much before is now replaced with an exciting sense of limitless possibility, having made it to the other side.

Gradually the rush of energy subsides. The experience cools, reflection now becomes possible and with it the opportunity to learn and to integrate the learning within our wider biography and life journey.

Helping someone through such a threshold experience requires great sensitivity. To push them too fast at the beginning, or to pull them to earth too hard later, can interrupt the process and damage the potential for learning.

Jean has been considering her future direction for some time. Following a holiday, she returned to work to find that the long awaited reorganisation had taken place and the work she was now doing was increasingly what she felt least interested in. Was this the time when she would take the step to find what she

wanted to do? No. Jean wanted to wait and see how things would work out, knowing just what that would mean, and even admitting to herself that this was a delaying tactic, putting off the need for her to take that step over the threshold of choice - the choice for her to do what she wanted. The threshold for Jean was not a particular job or a new type of work, it was giving herself the 'permission' to have the right to decide what it was she wanted to do and to go ahead and do it. Such a threshold was so crucially important that it would take her several months to ready herself for the step. When it came she was of course gaining a victory not only for herself about her work, but a victory for herself about the right to make choices for herself about the rest of her life.

She knew, at some level, that the consequences of making the choice over her work would have 'knock-on' effects upon the rest of her life and she wasn't ready to face those until she had prepared herself inwardly during the weeks that followed.

Liminality

Liminality is the term used to describe this free-floating boundary-less experience; the period, or the break between two phases; the 'in-between', which appears after one thing has come to a close and the next stage has yet to begin.

It is a period of suspension of the usual rules; of our sense of self and others; a marvellous and also a seductive space. New experience floods in and many new insights may follow. It is a time when a great re-ordering of our inner world takes place.

It is important that the help we receive at such periods enables us to harvest the greatest learning. Many of us, when we experience such a movement in ourselves, fear the reactions others may have and so keep the changes taking place to ourselves. Sadly, it often means that the process gets shut down or halted. If this happens we risk losing something valuable. Very often it is only through a sensitive exploration with someone experienced in such **inner journeys** that we can gain a sense of the importance of some of what takes place.

Liminality is the *'in-between'*. There is the time after the end and the time before the next beginning: these are the aspects of liminal space. Following a major transition or change, it is likely that an individual will spend a period of time disoriented and estranged from themselves, unsure and unclear about many things, even things not directly related to their change process. It may take time for the shifts to settle and subside. During this phase individuals are more vulnerable than they realise to *helpful* directions and suggestions from almost any source, since they have fewer internal references to help guide them.

Tim had been through a major change affecting his future direction and was now at a loss to explain how come he didn't feel more relieved that things were 'sorted out'. As he looked at this feeling of lack of energy, it began to dawn upon him that his mental landscape was, to some degree or another, undergoing some revision and he was not quite sure how it might all look once it had settled. He looked to the counsellor for help in this process, to give guidance and offer some landmarks. Fortunately the best he got was reassurance that it was O.K. to feel the way he was feeling. This was not the time to offer wise solutions or helpful advice or Tim might just take it. He needed the chance to let things find their own level.

Chapter Six

The Challenge of Change

Growth and Meaning

What each of us learns will vary according to the particular circumstances and conditions of background, culture and family values. Yet despite all this, Marris argues that:-

'The way anyone anywhere constructs the meaning of life is the outcome of a constantly developing, interacting set of emotional purposive and interpretive organisations, in which the experience of attachment has played so primary and crucial a part, that meaning without attachment is fundamentally inconceivable.' (P. xiv)

Conservatism as a Means of Defence

The anxieties which accompany any significant change often centre upon the struggle to defend or recover a meaningful pattern of relationships. Whenever people suffer loss, however much they may desire the change itself, they experience an internal conflict similar to that of grief.

Once it is recognised and acknowledged that the anxieties of loss are much the same, then the clinging and refusal which accompanies much social change (however benignly motivated by those proposing the change) and the ambivalence towards the *solutions* being offered becomes clearer.

Innovation and Change

Innovation, or self-generated change, follows the essential features of the loss and change model of Marris. Whilst on the surface there is a ready acknowledgement of the disruption that is a necessary element in bringing about the proposed change, there is also at work the effort to escape a deeper threat which will grow if the situation or relationship were to be left unchanged. The tension generated between the strain of change and the threat of things remaining too much the same produces similar reactions of ambivalence and anxiety that can be clearly observed in grief.

Assimilation of the Exceptional

The exception proves the rule we say. But if it means anything, it points to the fact that we would rather change our experience than our beliefs, rather try to find ways to make things fit what we already believe than change our beliefs themselves. We do it by avoiding information which contradicts our view (denial) and we do it by minimising the impact of what we do reluctantly concede. Changes in the structure of meaning are much slower than many people realise and much slower than planners ever account for.

What we can accommodate to is determined by the limits of our beliefs and beliefs are both conceptual and emotional. Together they are bonded into our **world view,** something we are attached to every bit as much as we are to the things around us.

The challenge of change for all of us lies in the need to revise our assumptions, however briefly, about ourselves, our relationships, and the world we live in. The effects of most changes are twofold. There are adjustments to what is termed our lifespace and to our assumptions.

Lifespace

The term **'lifespace'** describes our mental world. It covers our habits and routines, the predictable encounters of our day-to-day life, our assumed security and the familiarity of the environment we work in, the network of people that (very often) invisibly supports us and the financial and social security we rely on.

In any major change these things undergo some degree of review. Even positive change, such as moving house or getting a new job, requires some adjustment to our lifespace. The side-effects of even a positive change can be seriously disturbing. It may be in everyone's interest to get a bigger house, but once there it may well be that the family misses the old house more than expected. We can grieve for places every bit as much as for people.

The World of Assumptions

The term **'assumptive world'** is used to refer to the set of attitudes and beliefs we have towards ourselves and the world. These undergo challenge and review in the process of change. They include our notions of personal identity, our status, the place we have in other people's lives, our sense of purpose and our self-esteem. Again, even positive changes can bring painful side-effects. Taking on promotion at work often means, for example, being seen differently by others. No matter how little the person promoted feels they have changed, to be told you have become *one of them* may be a moment of painful recognition. Though you are still the same, no one else will actually act as if you are and it is now too late to go back. From now on you have to live out the implications of your choice.

Response to Change

The Chinese symbol for change carries the double meaning of both crisis and opportunity. Our reaction to change varies enormously within the same individual and between different individuals. Ways in which many people respond to the challenge of change are given below. An awareness of these ideas will be useful in extendng our understanding of the change process and enable helpers to be more effective.

Impairment of adaptive responses
The effort of responding to change lowers the individual's usual capacity to adapt to other, simultaneous changes.

Reduction of tolerance
This is the straw that broke the camel's back syndrome. Yet another change, even one of a minor kind, can be just too much for a person to take on. People who live at chronic levels of stress are often amazed at how such a little thing is the crunch point when they have been coping with a lot worse for years.

Rigidity in thinking
Some people become obsessive, quite unable to let go, have a break and then return to the issue. Their thinking and behaviour become grimly determined and flexibility goes. This may lead to tunnel vision: the inability to look outside for new perspectives in their desperate search for any solution. It may also mean foreclosing on options, rather than tolerating uncertainty any longer - any answer will do, even the wrong one, since at least that way the waiting is over.

From chronic to acute levels of response
If a person is already operating at chronic levels of stress, as further changes become acute they may become erratic and unpredictable in mood or behaviour and thus difficult to cope with or help.

Anxiety and panic
Some changes throw people into anxiety attacks, panic reactions, or dramatic games, all of which are simply ways of temporarily avoiding dealing with the situation.

Displacement in order to ignore or deny what is happening
Some people become over-committed to another safer area of life, usually only to postpone matters for a later time.

The Tasks of Change

There are two levels of self-management in working through change: the **emotional** and the **cognitive.**

The **emotional** task is to experience and come to terms with the emotional disturbance, the stress and the strain of the event. The **cognitive** task, meanwhile, is to make readjustments in understanding as a result of the implications of the change.

Progress in each of the tasks and in the different stages is rarely even. Different individuals at different times will be more focused in one area than another (trying to think their way through the change rationally at the expense of feeling any of it, for example) or they may become immobilised by the distress of the event.

When there is some progress in each area, the mover is likely to experience an increase in self-acceptance and personal autonomy.

Personal Influence Over Change

How far an individual is aware of a change and how far they feel they have a capacity to influence events will greatly affect their response to that change. But awareness of change and the capacity to influence it are, to a certain extent, self-determined.

There are those who take great responsibility for all that happens to themselves. They go out of their way to gather information and knowledge in order to help them cope with the events which lie ahead. Others do the minimum.

Consider, for example, the way different women respond to becoming pregnant. There are those who 'take it on', in the sense of becoming extremely committed to responding as fully as possible. They read, attend classes and clubs, follow their medical history carefully and so on. Other women respond much less actively.

What will be seen as a self-chosen experience by one person (and therefore one that they are able to influence) will be seen by another as an inevitable change over which they are powerless.

Figure 1 below illustrates a way of grouping events together using the two dimensions of awareness and choice. Events which are both voluntary and predictable are those to which people respond with the greatest flexibility, whilst events which are

	Voluntary (Choice)	**Involuntary (Lack of Choice)**
Predeictable AWARE	Promotion Marriage Entering College Buying a car	Paying Taxes Redundancy Retirement Ill-health Dying
Unpredeictable UNAWARE	Moving House Changing jobs Holiday Computer Dating Beginning a course	Sudden death of a parent/child/friend Divorce/separation Accidents Robbery Rape

Figure 1
PERSONAL CHANGE AND INFLUENCE

41

unpredictable and involuntary, such as an accident or being attacked, often leave individuals severely traumatised, sometimes for the rest of their lives. Traumatic change is unpredictable and involuntary, but it is important to remember that unanticipated and unpredictable elements are side-effects of all changes.

Some of the events in the figure above could appear in both the voluntary and involuntary 'sides'. Divorce or separation, for example, depending on the circumstances might be voluntary and an aware decision or the request for divorce could come as a shock and be very unwelcome, ie involuntary. The aim is to push the window back further and further into the 'voluntary / aware ' section. In this way we can see things coming and **choose** a response rather than endure effects we feel forced upon us. The writing which follows clearly illustrates this difference.

Martin and Adrian both worked for the same global organisation. They worked in different parts of the company in locations that were over 200 miles apart; but they occupied similar positions in the company structure. They were both rising middle managers.

Martin had worked for other organisations before joining the company in his mid-thirties. He had actively sought experience with them because he wanted to develop the breadth of his expertise. He was active in pursuit of his own career goals, so that when it first began to be discussed that the organisation might begin a massive programme of shedding staff, he considered his own position. 'I guessed it would be people like me they would want to elbow out,' he said. Rather than wait to be proved right, he approached the organisation and encouraged those responsible for the restructuring to consider him as dispensable - on the right terms.

The organisation welcomed his interest and composed a package of measures. Martin quickly realised all his hunches were correct. 'I was really fortunate to see the writing on the wall so early,' he said, 'because it meant that I was out there looking for the next thing to do with my life, enthusiastic and with a good deal of lead-in time before the thousands who came after me'

Many of those thousands of middle managers attempted to follow the footsteps of Martin - to go independent and become consultants. Few succeeded in the way Martin had.

Adrian, on the other hand, took a different route. He knew that the redundancies were happening. But he was initially unworried, because it affected those older than himself and in positions above him. 'At first it simply made my future look brighter. I saw all these guys eight or ten years older than I and they were making space for people like me to move into their positions.' Adrian was content to remain a company man. He had never worked for any other employer since leaving school. He felt that his loyalty to the company would be rewarded, whatever the changes.

Over the course of the following four years, he had many experiences that indicated that the company did not repay loyalty. The whole structure of the industry, as he knew it, was undergoing a revolution and in four years the company made over 80,000 people redundant or lost them through natural wastage.

It was only when his own department was being closed that Adrian even began to consider that it might reach him or leave him with a different future to the one he had decided would be his. 'It hit me too late that I was simply another brain too many. They didn't need my skills and they didn't want my contribution. And I should have recognised that months - years - before, but I didn't. I had got to that stage where I didn't even like much of the work I was doing anyway, but I was stuck in the rut by then.' He was forced out of the rut by redundancy. But now he was one of thousands selling his middle management skills and experience to a world that had them in over-abundant supply. He optimistically set out to sell himself and faced rejection upon rejection, before he began to face the deeply disturbing realisation that he had to rethink his future.

Adrian and Martin were not unalike in age, background, experience and expertise. Martin is not some go-ahead go-getter. He simply had an awareness about the trends that the future was following and acted upon them ahead of most of his contemporaries. Adrian was the reverse. He had no real thoughts about the future and even though he knew what was happening, he chose to overlook it and continued to believe in his own preferred version of events until it was too late to have much of a choice about what kind of future he might have.

Chapter Seven

Adult Life and Life Stages

Since Shakespeare and the *Seven Ages of Man,* if not long before, human society has been conscious that different life stages produce different challenges for both men and women. Our thirties differ from our fifties. Once through them, most people would not want to go back to their twenties. There are varied ways of characterising these stages and the one produced here identifies some of the major themes of each stage.

For example, not everyone settles down to establish a family between twenty-five and thirty-three: many in our society do it long before and some much later. Nevertheless this is the age when, for almost everyone, questions about settling down and having children are strongly present in their lives, whatever ultimate decision they make about it. And since it affects their peers as strongly, it provides an atmosphere for comparison and evaluation. 'How am I doing?' is often answered by looking around at how everyone else like me is doing. This affects how people manage change.

A helper may be tempted to point out to a woman who has just lost a child all the child-bearing years ahead, forgetting that to the woman concerned, future children do not compensate for the loss of this one. And part of the suffering is related to the fact that her peers do have the very children that she does not. The difference is felt all the more acutely and painfully in all the reminders of the loss surrounding her. This is something helpers should bear in mind when working with change and loss - how does the particular life-event mark the client out from those around them?

Life Stages

Adult life stage development is a relatively new field of interest in contemporary psychology. In the seventies Gail Sheehy wrote a well known bestseller entitled *Passages,* which outlined many of the typical crises of adult life. Part of the book's overwhelming success was its compilation of interviews from ordinary people who were facing predictable transitions and life changes. It seemed that in much of the Western world we had so concentrated upon the uniqueness of our experience that we had quite overlooked the familiarity of some of the changes individuals have to meet in the course of a lifetime. Many people opened the pages of *Passages* to find much valuable reassurance and help in explaining what was happening to them.

The Dutch writer, Bernard Lievegoed, wrote about the stages and phases of adult development in a series of excellent books. His own distinctive contribution to development studies was to include an overt sense of the importance of the individual's spiritual development alongside other aspects of development. He places a decisive importance upon the need for all of us to find some relationship between our outer and inner life. Anyone interested in thinking about these issues further should acquaint themselves with Lievegoed's work noted at the end of this book.

18-25 *Uprooting*

Once past, many of us remember our twenties as a distinctly insecure and uncertain time in our lives. At the time, they are often experienced as anything but tentative or provisional. And yet that is precisely what they are. It is the time of our first, uncertain steps on an independent life, a sense of personal identity and a feeling of having a separate self with which to meet the world.

Young people's views at this stage are often fiercely clear, with little room for shades of grey or any ambiguity. It can be a time of great energy for causes and for great self-sacrifice - work abroad or with the disadvantaged for example. There is energy and time and, usually at least, some money to begin constructing a life of one's own, whether it is lived within the old family unit, or with other peers. University, or a period as a student, often provides the first experience of living away from home. Relationships, whether casual or long lasting, are usually a source of intense interest and concern. Deciding what to do with one's life is an abstract but important question for this period, whether the jobs exist or not. Deciding what relationship to have towards money and success is often worked out in this period. Many people lay down pathways for themselves that lead into their late thirties only to find then that the life they have built does not really fit either themselves or their deeper values. They discover that they have simply lived out the peer ideas that were influential during this time in their lives.

This period, especially in a society undergoing the kind of social transformation described earlier, is one of testing out commitments, rather than engaging upon them. Ideas and interests may not survive for long. The individual needs time and experience to decide where they are to place themselves: to discover what kind of arrangements they need to suit the person they are only now discovering themselves to be. Having fall-back positions and keeping options open does not always appeal to the need for dedication that can come at this stage, but they are wise reserves to have to hand when some of the inevitable set-backs happen.

Main Themes

☐ Breaking the emotional links to the family of origin.

☐ Career exploration.

☐ Stabilising peer relationships and their importance.

☐   Managing one's own life; managing time and living space.

☐   Growing experience of solving one's own problems.

☐   Coping with the stress of changes and the buffeting of life.

☐   Periods of silence and growth of confidence, sometimes mixed with moodiness.

☐   Recognition that 'I am here and on my own' in some important respects.

Alec came for a series of counselling sessions that related to his being unsettled as a student. He couldn't concentrate upon his work load, and yet he knew he was bright enough to expect to do well. He wasn't sleeping and his anxiety was high. As the sessions progressed, he was anxious too not to go roaming over his childhood. He wanted the help to stay concentrated upon his present position. During one session he spoke of his sister and the difficulties she was having.

Alec was close to his sister. They had, it later turned out, shared a difficult childhood together and their relationship had enabled them to get through some of the worst of it. As a result of the closeness between them, Alec was unprepared for making relationships with other people without her. His life up to leaving for University had had people in it, interest and choices. It was only when he had to create these things for himself that he discovered how much he had always relied upon his sister providing the people, activities and interests in his life. His anxieties about his work were, in part, a response to his increasing fears about being isolated and lonely. Understanding it helped, but of course it didn't change the circumstances. Alec simply had never developed many of the social skills of his peer group and was all the more isolated as a result.

Understanding the position he was in did not mean it would be easy to remedy the situation. A series of weekend workshops where he deliberately went out of his way to meet people and learn about himself made a huge difference and proved a far more useful way of spending his time and money than talking about why he could not do what he wanted to do.

Many young people may well need the help of someone outside their situation to clarify concerns such as these as well as issues that are traumatic or disabling. Counselling can be of enormous benefit to such young people. But youth is to be lived. Too much counselling can be lost on the person if they are like Alec, without the relevant life experience they need to take part in their own lives. Counsellors should remember that referring people onto other activities is a useful strategy for some clients at some points in their lives, rather than have them talking about how they got to be the way they are.

23-30 Calming Down.
Having Second Thoughts.

The first steps into adult life have usually been accomplished at this time. Life is for real. The fact that this is not a dress rehearsal gradually begins to dawn upon us. We are living it and the way we are doing it is becoming a pattern. Do we like it? Does it fit us? Are the people who we find our life entwined with suitable to us and for us? Are the ways I spend my time satisfying enough to me? If not, then I need to begin to do something soon, or I may find this is the way I let it go on. Middle age can start here - if I am not careful.

The intensity of first relationships may have lessened, though not for everyone, and there may be more stability within friendship circles. Marriage may have been settled for many by this time. Work issues will have begun to formulate themselves into questions not so much of which career but which move within this career, or whether this is the time to begin a career search in earnest. Time to consider all options is not so freely available now. Contemporaries who settled down will be moving on; those who took time out will now be looking at the cost. Differences which seemed small only a couple of years ago can begin to open up between contemporaries at this stage: though these need not last for ever. There are some key questions which have to be met, if not resolved, during this time and the decisions, whichever way they go, are likely to have consequences for some time ahead.

In the earlier phase there was still time to reconsider, change and retreat, now the consequences of decisions begin to be recognised as having longer term implications. The impact of our choices grows as we begin to experience something of the weight of adult responsibility.

Main Themes

- [ ] Establishing a partnership or not.
- [ ] Career development and commitment.
- [ ] Becoming a parent and taking wider responsibility.
- [ ] Consumerism and home owning.
- [ ] Breaking psychological ties to the family of origin.
- [ ] Financial independence.
- [ ] Managing one's life, developing habits, routines and skills.

Bobby had enjoyed his teens and his twenties. He had had a succession of jobs and a succession of girlfriends. He was free of ties and he was not interested in settling down. At the sign of any relationship getting serious, usually if it lasted three weeks, this was a significant enough sign for him to begin to find

47

something problematic or unsatisfactory with it, or, more usually, the girl concerned. Very considerately and politely he would then break her heart and leave. He did not want to get 'too involved'. He had a wide group of friends that ranged across the social spectrum and he was welcome almost anywhere. This was part of his problem.

A life that was fine at eighteen was getting more and more uneasy at 29. More and more of his friends had settled down, though he could always find those who had tried it and it hadn't worked. Most of his circle had jobs that were paying better and providing the challenge of responsibility whilst he was still doing what he liked, often only for a matter of months. It wasn't that what he was doing was that dissatisfying or what they were doing was so appealing either, but he couldn't work out what it was that was making life seem less enjoyable than in the past.

Bobby was not going to find a counselling relationship easy either. He contracted to meet only for a short series of sessions. As he began to see the challenge for his life position, he began to realise that he might have some choices to make - one day. After all he did not want to get to forty and be like this. But for now, it was still fine enough not to need any more help, thank-you very much. Bobby wanted only to work out why he was feeling the way he was. He knew his life style would have to change as time went by, but it would be on his terms and only when he was ready and there was no magic day to be set for it. This, he realised, was all to do with growing up and settling down. 'And,' he pointed out, 'I'll be a long time grown-up. I'll stay this way for a bit longer now I know what it is I'm dealing with.'

28-35 *What's It All About?*

Often it is only as the major threshold of thirty approaches that individuals really find their independence. This may sound strange because long before then individuals will usually have left the family home and may well have an established family of their own. Nevertheless, it takes until about the age of 28 or so for the individual to experience themselves as a separate and responsible adult. It takes time living as oneself and being responsible for oneself to know what being **one's** *self* means. There are often faltering attempts to stand on one's own feet before this time comes around, but there are no more chances to try things out with a sense of youthful exuberance once this stage has passed.

Decisions have an importance by now and direction is unfolding. The consequences of the decisions made earlier are being reaped during this phase. Youthful enthusiasm or irresponsibility may now weigh heavily in the form of continuing commitments and expectations that go a long way into the future. Whatever illusions we have used to keep us enthusiastic in our job or in our relationships are likely to have been exhausted by now. We know the reality all too clearly and if we do not like what we see, or if we find the reality not what we expected, now is the time when deeper doubts and concerns begin to surface.

It may no longer be enough to compensate for a dull job with a good social life. It may no longer be possible to look ahead to remaining within a predictable relationship for the next thirty years. If there is a spark of ambition that has been put aside or ignored, now is the time it is likely to resurface and demand to be given some reconsideration. Others may look connected and settled and that may make one's own dissatisfaction all the more difficult to accept. The restlessness may find its way into inappropriate behaviour and out of character exploits. Affairs and wild business risks may be taken as a way of injecting some juice into life. Or a more sombre thoughtfulness may cast its way over everything leading the person to rethink what and who they are.

Main Themes

- [ ] Questioning the meaning.
- [ ] Re-evaluation of work, relationship and life.
- [ ] Success or not?
- [ ] A sense of, 'Where can I go?'
- [ ] Children growing.
- [ ] Hobbies often provide a new found sense of identity.
- [ ] Am I really here and what is it really like?
- [ ] What else is there?
- [ ] Managing my life and knowing more about who I am.

This is often one of the points in life that drives individuals to seek help. This decision may be the result of life somehow not fitting in with earlier expectations - a sudden interruption to a planned course of action; the breakup of a long relationship; a realisation that the work someone is doing no longer has enough heart in it; a sudden love affair or a serious illness. Often it is some shock to the sense of what life either was about, or could be about, that confronts the person with the need to re-examine their lives and their beliefs and their sense of who they are and what they want.

33-40 *Let's Get On With It*

The crisis may pass and the person find their way through the second stage of doubts. The inevitable crises and interruptions to a smooth life may be weathered and the thirties open out as a time for getting on with life once more. The disturbances usually fall away or a new start is made. Now is a time for strong energy to go forward. The conflicting demands of home, family and work are often easing off during this time, and the person may well make a renewed commitment to their working life or to their relationship.

The high flyers may be slowing down at this stage and those who have taken their time to move through their working life may well begin to catch up now. The benefits gained from steady work starts to bring its own reward, in terms of knowledge won from experience rather than theoretical knowledge gleaned from reading books or made up to fit the circumstances.

This can be matched with a renewed urgency to make the most of the remaining years of youthful vigour. At the same time, we know there is not indefinite time left to us. Whilst on the *outside* this may be a consistent period of steady commitment, it may be that the questions for the next phase are gathering force.

Main Themes

☐   Put the questions aside.

☐   Make another effort to make it all work.

☐   Chase success or a dream.

☐   Try to cram more into 'what's left' or 'what's here'.

☐   Conflict with adolescent children.

☐   More equal relationship with own parents.

☐   Adjust to the reality of circumstances.

☐   Consider making the best of it.

Nevil came for counselling because his wife thought it would be a 'good idea'. It had, he pointed out, 'helped her enormously' and they both thought it might be 'useful'. It seemed, as Nevil explained more of his life and circumstances, that his wife had taken over his life from his mother, who had done a very good job of ensuring that Nevil never had to think for himself about anything that might be considered emotionally challenging. His life was actually 'fine' and he didn't really know what difference talking to someone else might make, but he was prepared to 'give it a go' and see how he went on.

Needless to say it didn't go much further. Nevil was not choosing to be a client. He had little expectation of anything positive coming out of it and his life, as far he was prepared to look at it, was 'fine'. Whilst Nevil is not a typical client for counselling, he is an example of someone at that point in life who may often be looking for something, a new faith, a new interest, a new relationship, something to reawaken them to life, especially if they have felt alive in the past. It may be, as in Nevil's case, something of a half-hearted attempt to put their lives 'right' with a quick 'fix' from something.

The concerns that may bring someone into a counselling relationship need not always be immediate and dramatic. They can be a result of unease and vague dissatisfaction.

Nevil was not entirely satisfied with his life, as he was willing to admit, but he was not disturbed enough about any of it to feel the need to begin the process of change. Yet!

37-45 Oh No!

Here it comes; the **mid-life crisis** so often spoken of but never quite seen or understood - until it hits. Something that comes from out of the blue can strike at the very centre of life. An individual who has to date been a model of predictability and sobriety suddenly overturns the habits of a lifetime and throws in his job or starts an affair.

It is often a period of real discomfort and a sense of being at a loss for knowing what is happening to oneself or those around. All the landmarks seem to be cut adrift, either in succession, or all at once. We have to come to terms with the limits of what we are likely to accomplish and the sense of the finitude of our life - simultaneously. We will not go on for ever, but this job just might and then what will my life have added up to? It is a last time for facing oneself, recognising that each of us, however much we are blessed with others around us, is ultimately making the journey alone and that we have to answer for ourselves.

Those who have led a life that has fulfilled the expectations of others may now come to ask what they want for themselves and to wonder what it has all added up to - this life of putting others before themselves. Is there another chance to try again, take a last fling at life and sink all one's hopes and dreams in a new or another......? This may be an intense time viewed by others with a mixture of pity and despair, until of course it comes to their turn. For the truth is no-one escapes this phase, only some do not express themselves so dramatically.

Main Themes

- [ ] Mid-life crisis.
- [ ] The questions come back.
- [ ] The need to breakout.
- [ ] Another chance to ..... before it's too late.
- [ ] Career dreams fade - the reality is clear.
- [ ] Testing others and being tested.
- [ ] The search for meaning begins in earnest.
- [ ] Attempting new approaches and the risk of being ridiculed.

☐   A growing sense of being alone.

☐   Having to answer for oneself.

We have looked at several examples of people entering, or living through, aspects of the mid-life crisis earlier in this book. It is an intensely personal time since the crisis may take any number of forms, from a sense of disquiet and inward preoccupation all the way to dramatic outbursts of moodiness and provocative behaviour that has more in common with adolescence than mature years. For men it is often the facing of their own loss of power and physical abilities that they see coming to expression in their own children that brings about some of the painful confrontations between fathers and sons. It can be the strange mixture of protectiveness and envy of a daughter growing into her womanhood that can bring out the most erratic of authoritarianism from her father. Or it may arise out of work: a realisation that all one's dreams are far from being realised or a dispute gathers intensity. Whatever its origin and contributing influences, the mid-life crisis is often experienced as being at a distance from oneself, an observer enters one's own life and almost takes a disinterested curiosity in the anguish, the drama or the disquiet that is so often part of the background to everything. The elaborate **persona** that we assemble during our twenties, that we come to feel is who we really are, begins to crack in our thirties. Those things we have not allowed to have a place, those parts of ourselves that we keep well hidden, start to demand a place and start to wreak havoc in our lives if we do not grant them space and acknowledge their presence. It is this internal readjustment that makes the individual feel at once a victim to themselves and strangely out of control. It gives it a very disturbing quality and efforts to shut it down or close it off rarely succeed. It may drive it underground, but it rarely halts the process altogether.

For many women it is the onset of the menopause which brings the same questions to their attention and it is often a quieter more intense period of inner preoccupation. The moodiness may well express itself, but the concern over mortality and the ageing process, so powerfully experienced in her body, may be kept much more to herself, or managed by making light of it. Physical health is no longer something to be taken for granted and the energy available to do all those things that have been routine may now be there with less gusto.

'Man at the Mid-Point'
A short biography

I am forty-five years old. To understand how I've come to a point where I am embracing significant changes in my life it is essential to give a picture of my earlier life and examine the influences which brought me to a situation where change was not just desirable but inevitable.

I meet many people in the world I now move in who have arrived in some form of caring work via a life of pain, deprivation or hardship. If that is a qualification for the work then I am signally lacking in it. My childhood was spent on a farm just outside Leeds and my images of that time are almost exclusively happy ones. I loved my family and parents and they in turn loved me and brought me up in an atmosphere of strong but gentle caring. As a consequence, my progress through life has seemed pretty easy. Without ever really knowing what I wanted to do I drifted through school and into various jobs before settling with BT. Without trying too hard I rose to a middle-management position in the company and seemed set for, perhaps, one more promotion and then early-retirement at about 55 with a solid pension. Outside the company I had jointly started a theatre group which produced plays to a very high standard. I acted and directed and, latterly, started to write plays. I sang in an operatic society and revue group, I played golf and socialised well. I was very busy and hardly took time to look at what I was doing and how I felt about my life.

In all this time, the only blot had been the difficulties I had experienced in my relationship with my wife. Despite a lot of effort on both sides it seemed that we could not find a way to exist harmoniously together. Sexual and emotional issues led to relationships with other women, whilst my wife went off into her own place which steadily excluded me more and more. This started shortly after the birth of our daughter in 1981 and wended its way through to 1989.

My working life started to change in 1988 when I moved from a conventional management job in marketing to a new position as a facilitator - helping people comprehend and work with new ideas relating to the implementation of Total Quality. I fought very hard to get the job because I knew that it was the area of work I wanted to do - a chance to work in a helping rather than a commercially directed way. What I found as I embarked on the training was that it was very experiential and there was a lot of counselling basis. Much was made of Egan's book 'The Skilled Helper' and a great deal of the tutoring was 'hands off'. During the 3 full-week sessions away it became clearer to me that I had made the right decision and it also engendered a sense, almost, of invincibility (much needed as it turned out since my convictions about the rightness of what we were doing were not always shared by managers).

I worked in this environment, very happily, for 3 years. Then, at the beginning of 1991 I moved into a new division created from a re-organisation. Here I found myself 200 miles away from my line manager who was himself another 200 miles from his manager. The wide-area working, allied to a number of team and personal issues, contrived to leave me feeling trapped and vulnerable. When my boss refused to acknowledge my effectiveness (as evidenced by my customers) in my annual performance appraisal I felt in a dead-end in the work. The company was offering a very attractive redundancy scheme and it seemed to me that I had enough skills to sell on the open market; enough desire to get out from underneath the weight of working for them; and enough ambition to start working for myself in partnership with two others that I should take the risk. Curiously, it did not seem much like a risk. It felt very attractive and the only logical thing to do! During the last 3 months of my time at BT I had begun a skills training course as a beginning towards a personal goal of becoming a counselling practitioner - a journey I had decided to set out on some months earlier. I did not realise how much that would change my outlook and help me to see my life more clearly.

Things which enabled me to make the work change were the support of my wife, the support of the money and the pension at 60, and the ambition to go it alone. My wife and I at that time were enjoying a renaissance in our relationship which had almost reached divorce. Over time, I had confessed to affairs and she had admitted to her behaviour being difficult to live with. We were now moving steadily towards a renewed and, I believe, a strengthened future together. I had also been writing and had almost completed my second play as well as a number of short stories, snippets and songs. I determined that when I felt strong enough to face rejection I would submit these for scrutiny to publishers.

In the New Year of 1993 I started a second course where I would train to come within range of accreditation as a counselling practitioner. This was essentially an experiential course and required me to start off by examining my history and the main points in my life - in other words, biography work. I recorded all the good and bad things on a sheet of A3 and took them home. My wife picked up the folder looking for a loft layout I was drawing out and saw the biography work. In it there was sufficient detail about a relationship with a friend of hers and mine of which she was ignorant for her to decide over the following 4 weeks that this was the final straw and our relationship was over. This coloured a lot of my experience over the next 3 months, most of it being repetitious behaviour from other arguments in the past and a largely childish and hurt response from me about the way things had been recently and this wasn't fair - it was too long ago.

As I worked through the course, however, I began to think through why I was like I was and how the myths of belief and experience had set great boundaries around me. The main shift was engineered during some picture work I did. In looking forward to where I wanted to be I drew a field, trees, fence, open gate and large sun setting. It was a picture which sprang from my childhood and a memory of a perfect summer's evening on my father's farm. That it appeared at that time told me three things:
   * I wanted a return to the freedom of that time
   * I wanted to learn again about being solitary but not alone
   * I wanted to get back in touch with nature to which I had been so close

Actually, it told me more, as I discovered over the next few months.

I learned as I moved further into my journey that I wanted to celebrate the strengths which I had inherited from my father. I had become more aware whilst doing my biography work how much I respected as well as loved him, and recognised how much of his depth of love I had inherited. In the same period I also realised how I had shut out the influence of my mother since her death in 1971. My abiding image until this time had been of her wasted body lying in her bed in the terminal stages of cancer. It was not a picture I wanted to bring to mind so I guess I suppressed it and, in the process of doing that, effectively switched off my recognition of her contribution to me. Through working with a counsellor I have now replaced that image with one of her wrapping me in a warm bath towel at the age of six or so and hugging me close. That summed her up. She gave love selflessly to her children and expressed it warmly in a host of different ways every day of our lives. I have also learned to celebrate my legacy of nervous energy which I believe I receive from her. The creative, musical part is her particular gift and that is very important to me.

The picture also showed me that there was a gate, it was open and I had an opportunity to walk through it. This meant some sort of change to me and it was concurrent that at the time I drew the picture I was emerging from the worst mental turmoil in my married situation. I had experienced a very low point which I had likened to being in a black cellar, trapped in a vat of oily liquid and this was filling up to overflowing, during which process I was likely to be drowned. Over the next month, the experience with the picture helped me to create a new vision for myself. This was that I had escaped from the cellar (with one mighty bound he was free!) and was walking along a lit corridor towards an open door. The corridor was light and there were traps and obstacles to negotiate but the brilliant light at the end was an unmissable goal. In the next three months I found myself settling my mental debts, as it were, with the result that I stood on the threshold of the door (the gate in my picture?) and then walked through.

In the process of arriving at this state I had taken a hard look at my situation at home and decided that I would stay with my wife and children for as long as we could make it work without impairing our own and their lives too much. I knew I would know when that dividing line was crossed and I also knew that I would not retreat from the decision when it came, even though I also knew it would be hard for me to do it. I also took a hard look at my work situation and affirmed my commitment to both achieving accreditation as a counsellor and pursuing a line of work which encompassed training in change principles and active efforts to sell my writing. In summary I found that, after 27 years of working to no particular goal, I had found a vocation; something which had meaning and purpose to me.

This is where I am now. The picture is by no means complete. I know I still have many hurdles to cross. I have much work to do to shake off some of my more persistent limitations. I still find it hard, for instance, to say how I feel at the time I'm feeling it. Usually this is because I can't do it in my normally articulate way and I feel exposed and childish if I let it out as it comes. Consequently, I tend to sit on my feelings. I also find it difficult to express myself effectively in groups of more than seven or eight in a personal way, which is part of the same problem as well as one of feeling overwhelmed by large groups.

The difference from the past is that I want to take on the challenge. I want to explore and develop the person I am towards the person I want to be. Like most people I want to be liked but the changes I've experienced means that this is not at the cost of inhibiting myself. I am involved in a process of internal growth where I want to arrive at a state in which I can celebrate my own strength and give to others the benefits of the learning I have received during my journey.

When I first knew what it was like to have certainty it felt as though something entered my body. It was like a transfusion of excitement which bubbled and coursed through every part of me. It took me back to the time I was eleven or twelve, sitting in my father's field on a summer's evening, looking at the oak tree at the far end; the fields surrounding me; the pine wood skirting one side; rabbits playing near the fairy-ring of toadstools near the oak tree; the seagulls and crows screaming and coughing; the gate in the corner of the field open. I felt so at peace then, so sure of my future, so happy. That's how I feel now.
Geoff Walker

43-52 *Quieting Down*

Once we have faced our own mortality and the recognition that we ultimately have to work it out for ourselves and nothing can, in the end, enable us to escape ourselves, we are left once again with the consequences and the choices about what we are to do; how we are to do it and who we want around us. A renewal of affirmation for more enduring values returns. Money often becomes less important at this stage. Life becomes more stable and we can often take the time to listen to our internal voice as well as external demands. This can be a time of deepening connections, as the passing interests and temptations of the past are seen against a longer perspective.

This is often a period of deep fulfillment and thankfulness for the satisfactions that are to be found in the day to day events of life, for the simple contact of a deep relationship and for those moments when life simply fits together in unexpected and delightful ways. There can be space and energy to give to others who are struggling with some of the issues that are now beginning to lie in one's own past. Compassion may begin to take on a new meaning as a result of the sufferings one has had to meet face to face.

Main Themes

- [ ] Making the most of it.

- [ ] Stamina and endurance to contribute.

- [ ] Children no longer so central.

- [ ] Time for oneself and others.

- [ ] New ways of relating to ageing parents needed.

- [ ] Enjoying the rewards that come with this stage.

- [ ] Awareness of physical prowess, changes in strength etc.

- [ ] A deeper contact with the self.

Simon had been a successful career man. He had risen through his talent and ambition to a relatively senior position in a substantial company. He had fought his boardroom battles to establish himself as a man to be reckoned with. He was, however, sensitive and artistic in his interests and he had not given over his life to work alone. He had resolved the issues in mid-life by crashing on with his career ambitions. In other words, he had not resolved anything. He had wrestled with and fought himself into submission and he was in charge, not only of his own will and the company he ran, but his life in general, or so he thought.

Simon represented the interesting example of the consequence that can all too easily occur if the mid-life crisis is not faced and worked with. By battling it out with himself, Simon had reasserted his old self over the forces that were attempting to seek expression in his life. He had been successful but at what cost?

Those forces were not gone. They were buried and from time to time they would haunt him - at moments he least expected it. This made his judgement sometimes faulty and his command of the situation less trustworthy. It was 'nothing to worry about' he said, as though to reassure himself and since he wouldn't admit his doubts to himself there was only one way to go and that was for the errors to increase. The poor decisions grew in number until gradually he had to recognise that he was in a war of attrition with himself and he was not winning. Unless he did something quickly he began to realise that he would take one decision too many and risk something crucial. Drinking as much as he did, he began to admit, was all part of the strategy for managing himself through his difficulties.

Simon had to face his 'inner demons'. He not only had to begin to find ways to manage his present circumstances, but to come to some kind of relationship with those other aspects of himself that he had been so strongly denying by fighting. The work would become more complex and challenging as a result.

50-60 *The Mellow Time*

Now comes the time for evaluations and assessments. There are the beginnings of realising that what we have made is what we have to measure ourselves against. There is still time ahead to accomplish much, but not the high points of our youth. Our value is now likely to be as a source of experience and practice wisdom rather than dynamic effort. The ego is less important at this stage - for most - though if the ego has been a strong force in a person's life they may have found it difficult to adjust to the inevitable physical limitations which everyone becomes increasingly aware of during this period. Retirement approaches and another major adjustment into a new phase of life has to be contemplated. For many, retirement is imposed during this period and they find themselves little prepared for the major upheaval that results to life-style and relationships. The abrupt shift to a leisure-based way of life can be traumatic for many.

Main Themes

- [ ] More time for self.
- [ ] Work and home come into balance.
- [ ] Rewards from past effort reaped.
- [ ] Prepared to take things more leisurely.
- [ ] Companionship replaces spending on leisure.
- [ ] Enjoy it whilst you can.

Sheila had been a successful manager in a large organisation. She had had a long career and was well thought of. This should have been the mellow period of her career, however the organisation re-structured and there was no longer a place for Sheila within it. At the very stage when she had so much to give back by way of experience and wisdom, the company was saying she was not needed. It left her with strange and contradictory feelings. It was clear to her that she had been valued and the package she was offered was 'more than generous' but it didn't incline her to feel satisfied.

As we worked together, it became more and more evident that what Sheila was being denied was the opportunity to put back anything of the long experience she had acquired. Denial of this opportunity to develop others and take a more leisurely role in organisational life had left her feeling emptied. And the chance to evaluate and consider what her career had added up to was also being taken from her. She was being made to *finish* before she was ready to end. Much of her need to resolve issues about the scope and the purpose of her work and how she had seen it develop over almost three decades was not going to take place amid the continuing participation in company life, but from the distant

reaches of an early and enforced retirement.

Many organisations fail to realise that this stage of reassessment and completion is important, indeed essential for employees, but it is also important for the organisation to have the contribution of the elders left behind as part of the history of the work - unless of course you deliberately want those memories to be erased

60 Plus The Autumn Period

The later stages of life begin with retirement and the withdrawal from such an active role in the world and one's community, in favour of a return to the narrowing horizons of one's immediate circle. There are financial curbs to one's wishes and fewer occasions to take risks. If prepared for, of course, this can be a great flowering of later life, when long awaited ambitions can be fulfilled with a sense of time to take it in. Health issues which may have been a problem at different points in the past, may become a major concern or preoccupation. Without a sense of purpose - that now has to come from inside - individuals may well find themselves feeling used up, with little motivation to make the most of this new period of life.

Main Themes

Withdrawal from work orientation.

Financial constraints.

Facing ageing and loss.

Questions about personal health.

More time available.

Re-evaluation of life experience.

Give ground to children or others.

Face death.

Take an interest quietly.

Geoffrey had held a post in an educational institution that he had loved. His work had been rewarding. Helping young people learn had been a life's work that had brought pleasure and satisfaction. The approval and respect of colleagues a fitting tribute to his achievement. He had planned his retirement and looked forward to it. He had enough money and mobility to do those things he liked and to travel when he wished. He had been ready. Until it happened.

It took many months of growing unease before he entered a counselling relationship, he reflected in the early sessions, because he felt that it wasn't anything to do with retirement - he was so well prepared. Only with reluctance did he realise that however well he planned for it and however many opportunities he enjoyed with the time and space to take them up - retirement was a different land from any other he had previously visited. Getting used to what it meant was not something, he realised, he could anticipate from the familiar and fulfilling position of the last months of his working life. Many questions were being raised now that it was here: questions about the present and how to manage it; questions about the future and what might lie ahead, but questions about the past too, more than he had ever thought or expected.

For Geoffrey, retirement became an active period of psychological and emotional exploration; at first painfully difficult - he had spent a lifetime as a thoughtful but not so introspective a man, struggling with his own ambivalences and confusions, reassessing his relationships, considering again what his marriage meant, how he had been as a father and through many, many questions. Initially, much of it was something of a struggle, but there was sufficient reward in it for Geoffrey to continue. Gradually he became more and more familiar with himself and more and more fluent in how to be with himself. Retirement was another point of take off for Geoffrey, an important stage of his development that he might never had entered had it not been for his expectations being unfulfilled.

Themes and Stages

Clearly this list of themes is neither unique nor exhaustive. There are others which could be selected. They are, however, representative of the kind of issues people face at different stages in their lives.

The value of such a framework lies in being able to draw upon it to help an individual locate themselves within the range of issues they might be facing at any particular time.

For example, to be a woman alone in her mid-thirties, following the end of a partnership, however painful, is not usually experienced in the same way as it is for a woman in her forties and at the onset of menopause. A man thrown out of work in his thirties will tend to come back into life more quickly than someone who has reached 50. These are stereotypical examples, given to illustrate the point that, in part, how we experience what is happening to us is shaped by where we think we are in relation to other people around us, the age that we have reached and the life expectations we have acquired.

Each life stage is marked by a crisis point, a pivotal time of vulnerability and potentiality during which we can go forward to develop deeper capabilities, or find ourselves overwhelmed and defeated - too injured and debilitated to begin the next phase. There are key tasks to engage with at each stage and how successfully we meet and resolve these tasks shapes what resources, insights and understanding we bring to the next.

There is an external element to many events - ceremonies, routines, rituals, official papers to sign and so on. They hold an important significance: they are the public sign of what has happened. They give public recognition to new status, for example, but it is much more how an event is carried within an individual that determines its personal significance.

Adult Identity

Part of our adult task is to establish how far we are willing to respond to the various calls on our allegiance; family, job, class, community, we have to work these out. Where do we belong? How much do we belong? And to what do we belong? At the same time, we have to develop our personal values, decide the extent of our contribution and purpose and establish our own goals through our participation in the world. The tension between our outer and inner world is resolved differently by each individual. How we do it; what we avoid; what we accomplish and so on are all indicators of our growth.

Managing many of these changes is turbulent, unsettling and sometimes frightening (whatever other people may tell us). Regression, accommodation and periods of stagnation are all likely before any long term integration is accomplished.

The optimal potential for growth occurs when the challenges a person has to meet are slightly beyond their present coping skills, so that they have to stretch themselves, and yet not so much beyond them that they are overwhelmed or forced to withdraw.

Section I
Recommended Reading

Berne, E	*Sex In Human Loving* Penguin	1970
Bly, R	*Iron John* Element	1990
Ferguson	*The Aquarian Conspiracy* Paladin	1980
Handy, C	*The Empty Raincoat*	1994
Houston, R & Goodchild, C	*We Two* Acquarian Press	1992
Keen, S	*Fire In The Belly* Piatkus	1992
Keen, S	*The Passionate Life* Gateway	1985
Large, M	*Social Ecology* Hawthorn	1981
Lievegoed, B	*Phases* Rudolf Steiner Press	1979
Lindfield	*The Dance Of Change* Arkana	1986
Schutz, W	*Profound Simplicity* Turnstone Press, London	1979
Taylor, B	*How Did I Get Here?* OASIS Publishers	1994
Taylor, B	*Where Do I Go From Here* OASIS Publications	Autumn 1995
Toffler, A	*The Third Wave* Bantam	1981

Section II

Loss, Grief, Bereavement, Death and Dying

Death in life

The fear of death is intimately related to fears of the loss of the physical self. Ultimately what we fear is the end of our physical existence. Our body is the home of death.

We too easily think of the body as the abode of life, but until we have accepted the body and its ageing - the visible sign of our mortality - then we cannot fully embrace either our living or our dying.

We avoid the body because it reminds us of our frailty and impermanence. The fear of death, through the fear of the body's physical dissolution, can mean that we come to live a perpetual spiritual death. Seeing no further than our physical form, we cannot bear to think of what death is.

But there is no need to fear death.

What should be of most concern to us is that we fully live the life we have, rather than live under the shadow of the fear of death, or act from behind whatever facade we have adopted. What matters most is the discovery and expression of our potential. Then we begin to act, unafraid of being caught out because we do not live up to the expectations of others, or the image we have of ourselves. To the extent that we take on the roles and expectations that surround us, and come to live through them, we are already, in a vital respect, dead. By living out what we think we ought to do we become trapped and unable to realise our own potential. To reject this way of living, however, means to contradict much of what we have come to believe and rely upon.

Chapter Eight

Memory and Suffering

Memories

An important feature of our lives is our memories. Experience may be all that we have now, but our memories enable us to turn our experiences into different versions of history that we create for ourselves and which helps create a sense of authorship and influence over what happened to us and how we understand it.

It is important, when looking back on events, to remember how the mind weaves different patterns and learns different things according to the needs of the individual and the time. In an important way we create our own sense of the past. For some it is a rich source to return to, capable of yielding treasures on any occasion. For others the past is a bitter place - they cannot find solace, they cannot find peace and they cannot find inspiration.

Each of us constructs our own past. This does not mean that the experiences we have are unimportant, or that all experiences can create an equally simple past; it is not as easy as that. But our memories, however different, are the basis for the way in which we go back to the past and gain sense and understanding from it or not.

'Stuck' Memories

If we are stuck with obsessive pictures that we cannot let go of; if we are constantly returning to bitter memories that we are not willing to learn from; if we are bound by beliefs or rules that prevent us from being released from our past mistakes; or if we are hampered by an image of ourselves that twists every experience into yet another example of how we have failed: if we do these things with our past, then our past will reward us in kind.

Sometimes we do learn how to look at those things that for so long we have been unable to because the hurt and pain were too great. The day comes when we see those events again, from a new place, and begin to see them differently, take them less seriously. They begin to lose some of the powerful feelings associated with them.

Sometimes we look back, realising how unimportant an event actually was and how much false, inflated importance we attached to it. There are those other memories we do not want to go back to, and when we do, we certainly do not want to understand what is there to be found, because that would force us to change. It would mean our having to grow and move on, and, for whatever reason, we do not want to do that, at least not yet.

There are people for whom life does not make sense anyway and therefore the past is absurd. For them anything goes. Since nothing matters the past is also irrelevant.

Some only want to keep the listener by their side, or to convert the helper to their own sense of pointlessness that they have found for themselves. If we create our own past and decide that everything is absurd, it is a choice and right that we have. Helpers, however, need to recognise when they are being invited into such a game.

Aspects of Suffering

We can think of suffering as having four distinct levels: **physical, emotional, mental and spiritual (or existential).**

Physical Suffering

The sheer pain an individual may be in can distort, cloud or even obliterate all else. Consciousness can become focused on the pain, tracing its patterns, awaiting the next attack and so on. Such physical pain may well severely impair, or even remove completely, any ability to concentrate on other aspects of life.

Physical pain is often the most obvious to recognise and the easiest to do something about. In recent years improved methods of pain control have done a great deal to help thousands of people.

Physical care can, however, become the focus of help at the expense of other equally important aspects of individual suffering. But effective pain relief without other help will not be sufficient in dealing with overall suffering.

Emotional Suffering

Emotional distress can manifest itself in many ways. We all experience grief and sadness, or the sharp anguish of failure. Our emotional make-up is a powerful influence throughout the whole of our lives and all of us have areas of our feelings that we manage less well than others.

There are many ways an individual gets locked into their emotions, becoming stuck, unable to release their feelings and move on. This may take the form of exaggerated reactions, sullen withdrawal, or other extreme responses.

Feelings themselves have no urge to permanence. They can be let go of, but having held on to them for so long may make an individual fear losing control - the very thing they may need to do (with the support and care of another person attending to them.)

Alternatively, others may need to recover a degree of direction and expression over feelings which have become a chaotic bundle, likely to explode at any time. Such random outbursts of feeling help no-one, least of all the person expressing them, since real support and genuine care are the last things they inspire. Helping such a person find a safe place to work through their feelings, rather than just mopping up after their outbursts, may be essential.

It is important to remember that people can be victims of their feelings just as much by not expressing them as by over-indulging. Those feelings which remain unexpressed are merely far easier to overlook.

Mental Suffering

Mental torment over situations long since gone; the anguish of being constantly haunted by words you wish you had never said; the sense of failure that a recurring memory brings with it, are all ways of suffering mentally. Fear, guilt and shame are typical underlying influences that can generate mental suffering. When there is no more I could have done, it may still leave me wishing I could have done more. That may easily turn into a belief that I **should** have done more, resulting in guilt that I did not.

We live in a society with very firm rules about how we ought to behave which often causes mental anguish for those who have done their best and still failed. This is why talking with others who can put a realistic perspective on it all can help restore our own view of things and lead to us forgiving ourselves. People locked in fear, guilt or shame may stay stuck, unable to move on or contribute to others. It can be a sad waste when a person refuses to forgive themselves for something they did (or did not do).

Spiritual Suffering

Torment about the lack of any important spiritual understanding may have an enormous effect on how a person copes with grief and loss. For some people, their spiritual beliefs are a guiding light that enables them to endure the most tragic of losses. For others they are a rack that stretches them beyond breaking point. In a society such as ours, where spiritual values and questions of deeper belief are not always spoken of freely, many people have had little opportunity to talk through what they believe and understand life to be, or the part they have played in it.

All of us have a story to tell that makes up the life we have lived. All of us need time and space to understand the contribution we have made, and the mistakes we have made too, in order to gather a sense of what we have accomplished. Without it, life becomes fragmentary and meaningless. Sadly, that is often how it is for all too many people.

Others have the anguish of their spiritual longings being left unfulfilled, because they either could not ask for, or did not get, the help they needed in time. The lack of opportunity to become reconciled to the life that has been lived may create suffering every bit as grave as that of any other kind.

The piece of writing included here was written by someone who almost without warning had to face chronic pain over a matter of months. Little was known about the condition which brought about the pain except that it generates severe pain in the face. For weeks the pain continued, only occasionally reducing to bring temporary relief. There was a period when the pain left and it looked as though the condition was going to improve. Within a couple of weeks it returned. The pain has now been present almost uninterrupted throughout a period of six months. We have spoken together and worked in different ways to help manage the pain, face the pain, ease the pain, ask questions of the pain. It has been difficult work, but in amongst it has been some yield of understanding and growth for Rachel Clare. This piece of writing is one such example.

You hate me and would disown me - yet, I exist.
You hate me since you cannot control me and have your own way. Yet the only power I have is that with which you invest me. If you would but surrender your grip on me, let me be and not fight against me, you would find in me something of your own underlying nature.
Trust me: learn to trust me and let me show you part of the richness of life.

You fear me since you let me divest life of its meaning and depth, and you fear that life itself - as you know it - may disappear. Yet you could make me work for you and add meaning to your life.

I can break you into pieces, or I can break you open so that the buried seed of your life stands open to the sun. Open to allow it to grow and mature and eventually to bear fruit.
Then your fear would be understandable. Fear of what this situation is asking of you; of where it might be leading you.

You fear being useless, or perhaps more honestly, you fear being thought of as useless. What you do has become too important. I can show you that life still carries on, even when I have stripped you of all that you thought important; all that bolstered up your self-image. Life is more than this.

You tend to identify with me. When will you learn how much bigger than me you are? I am only a part of the totality of your life. If you could but learn this, you would discover something of the depth of life.

Trust me. Learn to trust me and LIVE.

Chapter Nine

Attachment, Separation, Loss and the Maintenance of Meaning

If we become greatly attached to someone or something we may fear that the loss and subsequent separation from them will be unbearable. Some people learn not to trust that anything will last 'long enough'. They therefore do not let themselves get too attached to anyone or anything; often they are deeply unhappy. But there are others who cling desperately to almost all attachments. They seem to throw themselves into things - relationships, work, hobbies or whatever - with a passion that borders on madness. They too are often unhappy, because, sadly, they find too few people can return affection with the intensity they crave, or can cope with their own overwhelming need for attention.

The Influence of Childhood

It is largely as a result of our upbringing that we develop our characteristic patterns of dealing with attachments and separation. Parents provide the base of safety (or lack of it) from which the child can explore their widening world. This helps determine the **affectional bondings** that we develop throughout our lives. Good, strong attachments do not overlook the possibility of loss or separation. Through experiences such as losing toys, pets and friends, the child learns to cope with loss and yet still retain a sense of trust.

Over-protected children may suffer the inevitable losses of life with exaggerated reactions, which can lead to complicated responses in adult life when coping with serious losses. Unskilled parenting can lead to over-anxious attachments.

Facing separation and loss can be experienced as a deep pain of rejection and hurt that is akin to being abandoned. However much the end of an unhappy relationship may be wished for, when it does come there is still the pain of separation and the emptiness that goes with it. However much of a mercy it is when an older person dies after a long and painful illness, there are still feelings of being robbed of the opportunity of ever seeing them again. These feelings may be momentary or long lasting.

Irreplaceable Loss

Some people find the loss of a particular person or relationship enough of a reason never to recover. Their life from then on is lived out against the background of this irreplaceable loss. For others, it may be years before they can risk another close attachment after losing one earlier in life. The greater the potential there is for loss, the more intense the individual's reaction is likely to become, and **the response to irretrievable loss is grief and anger.**

Responses to Loss

Responses to loss and the news of loss are often complicated because of the confused mixture of the reactions they raise. In our society, it is expected and allowed for people to feel sad at a loss, but to express anger can bring criticism and disapproval. Yet part of loss is the very real sense of personal hurt, the feeling of being rejected, or even abandoned, that accompanies the absence of someone we care about.

Such feelings are not *rational*, but they are natural; rarely are they encouraged. This denial of our own *selfish* need to experience the pain of being let down and to feel lost is not useful, but it is all too common and it keeps the sufferer from experiencing the whole range of feelings and emotions that loss provokes.

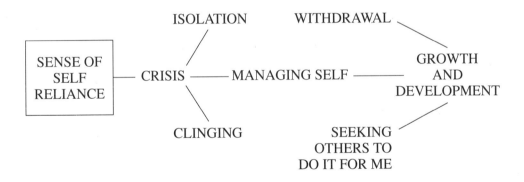

Figure 2

DEPENDENCY NEEDS AND CRISIS REACTIONS

A simple way to think about these aspects of loss comes out of looking at loss in relation to dependency needs. We are all born totally dependent on those around us. Gradually, through parenting and the influence of other important figures who respond to our growing efforts to master our world, we acquire a sense of who we are and what we can do. We begin to show signs of self-reliance.

| Infancy Childhood Adolescence | Maturity | Mid Life ———————► Increasing |
| ◄——— Dependency ———► | Independence | Self Reliance ———► Dependency |

Figure 3

LIFE STAGES

But we do not make that journey as a simple straightforward projection. Experiences may occur which make us feel that it is unsafe ever to trust in ourselves, or others, about certain aspects of life. Some children are given such erratic and unstable experiences that they find it difficult to trust strongly in anything or anyone. So they grow up with a relative sense of dependency that functions more or less satisfactorily, until some major crisis occurs to shake it. Then they may display fewer independent and adult reactions than they might like.

There seems to be two extreme reactions, and a range of variations between them. There are those who fiercely reject help and prefer withdrawal and isolation, and there are those who look for someone to cling to at any price, someone to help them cope, or even to do the coping for them.

Of course many people switch between these two positions at different times, making them complain at those doing their best to offer support, which is therefore rejected. Helpers may leave well alone, only then to be told that they do not care. Realising that you will not be thanked for your best efforts during a crisis and simply getting on with the job in hand is a sign of a mature helper.

Loss and Change

Loss, change and separation are inevitable and universal processes linked to the human experience of attachment and grief. And though the forms of loss may vary according to culture and background the underlying human experience is the same.

Our response to change is never straightforward, no matter what we like to think. It is paradoxical: now eagerly expecting it, only to feel a rushing disappointment later. Feelings fluctuate, making any clear straight line impossible - though many of us become frustrated with ourselves for not behaving in a more controlled fashion. Why should it be that change, even positive change, should be accompanied by such fluctuating and contradictory emotions?

In part, at least, it is that all change confronts us with two opposing impulses:-
- the need to accept whatever the losses are which accompany the change, if we are to move on

versus
- the natural desire to linger on in the hope of recovering that which is being lost, or of finding ways to include those aspects in a new situation that we do not wish to lose.

The more we put off facing up to loss, the more energy we expend in denying what is happening, pretending that it doesn't matter, or minimising the effects, the more difficult it is to face the full consequences of the loss when hope finally gives out altogether and we have to recognise the inevitable.

Our assimilation to any serious loss is slow and painful. Hurt is an inevitable part of the process. It is something nothing and no one can take away. Helping people face the pain of loss requires compassion and an inner clarity that ensures we can remain present with the sufferer, but open to them, not attempting to do their suffering for them or making superficial efforts to 'make it alright'.

Key Conditions Affecting Loss - Our Childhood Experience of Attachment.

The more complicated, or difficult, our relationship to that which is lost, the harder it is likely to be to rebuild future meaning in a way which can separate the emotion and the purpose from the irretrievable circumstances. If we meet a major loss having had the experience of poor or inadequate attachments in the past, then our ability to work through the effects of a loss will be more problematic. The less opportunity to prepare for the loss, where the loss is unpredictable or without overt meaning; the more traumatically will the event be experienced and the more damaging will be its effects upon the individual's overall structure of meaning. The more something matters to us, in other words, the more insecure future attachments are likely to become. When a loss is sudden, unforeseen events following the loss may support or frustrate efforts to work out the ambivalent impulses.

Bereavement as an Example

If we take bereavement as an extreme example of loss and change, then it is not simply the question of making good a lost relationship, or coming to terms with a death within the context of a life that will continue undisturbed and go on making the same kind of sense that it always has - but that all meaning is called into question, because the meaning and purpose of life itself is based upon our important relationships (whether they are good or bad relationships is not the point here).

For the bereaved partner; children, home, work and social network have formed the context for a relationship which no longer exists. The reminders and effects are present everywhere and felt everywhere. To begin the search for new meaning at a time when all previous meaning is in question is arduous, painful, erratic and uncertain. It is a time when all landmarks are gone and all signs are unreliable.

Grief

The reaction to this state of affairs is usually called grief and all loss produces some measure of it. Generally speaking, the more a change disrupts a pattern of meaning,

71

the greater will be the experience of grief and the longer it will take to resolve. The need to adjust both to a new set of circumstances and to a new sense of meaning is similar in social change to that in bereavement.

Attachment and the Development of Purpose and Expectation

Purposes and expectations form around all the significant aspects of our day to day life, our work, friendships, leisure activities and so on. In part they create the routines and the structures that make up the pattern of our life as we know it. Whenever these things are threatened by change, the structure of meaning that is attached to the activity or relationship undergoing the change becomes de-stabilised. This may well have a *knock-on* effect upon other aspects of our life. We may well begin to think that, 'If this part of my life is suddenly vulnerable, maybe other parts are as well.' The result can take the form of wide-spread anxiety, restlessness and the sense of unrealistic despair that nevertheless is all too real.

The Importance of Meaning

The need for meaning, to make sense, to understand is a crucial organising principle for human beings and their behaviour. Through this need we structure our experience and relate our purposes and our expectations in order to organise our activities. We make sense of all that happens to us by the meaning we ascribe to it, whether or not it 'means' anything in any objective sense at all. When we cannot find reasons for an event, we usually experience confusion, withdraw and become preoccupied. Life without meaning is unbearable.

Attachment

Our response to change is fundamentally influenced by the quality and reliability of our attachments. By the time a child has reached somewhere between four and six months his or her attachment behaviour is well developed and so is a fear of strangers.

It is the continuity and stability of the nurturing figures who create the basis for a predictable response. The absence of such continuity and stability may undermine an individual's sense of stability for life. The major task of the child is to make its attachment relationships relatively secure so that a sense of environmental security can begin to establish itself (other people being, in this sense, part of the environment). As maturity approaches we gradually reduce the need for the original source of love and security to provide it and instead begin to look to those we meet in our friendship groups and so on to offer it to us and receive it from us.

Attachment in this sense is **'neither an emotion nor a purpose but a condition'** (Marris Pxiii) out of which emotion and purpose arise. Depending upon the security of our earlier attachment bonds, we develop our individual predispositions to become attached in later life to appropriate and available figures. With attachment goes the accompanying feelings of comfort, anxiety, anger, joy. Ambivalence is then inherent in all attachment and coping with ambivalence leads people to devise strategies to minimize the disturbance. These may take the form of **denying** difficult elements which don't fit the picture that we would like to see, or it may lead to our **revising our assumption about the importance of the relationship itself.**

Establishing Meaning

The universal human need to seek meaning and the very individual and particular experience we have of attachment behaviour during our early years, establishes life-long patterns of *sense-making,* of understanding cause and effect, of predictability, of personal effectiveness, of a sense of order, relevance, purpose and how we approach getting what we want - to name only a few consequences.

In order to establish the meaning of anything we have to identify, classify and compare present experiences and relationships according to their fit from past experience. The confidence to explore experience and seek new meaning is a direct result of the security of our early attachments, which in turn is largely influenced by how far our early attachment figures encouraged us to explore and therefore rewarded us.

Genuine independence arises as a result of the approval we gain from those who love us and self-reliance develops out of being able to trust in the love of those responsible for bringing us up. If there is a continuing consistency in the way we grow up the more we will expect to meet secure attachments in the future.

The Development of Meaning

As we develop, we are increasingly encouraged to make sense of our experience by seeing it *in frames,* which highlight particular elements or features of experience, according to the context in which we find ourselves. 'Traffic lights', for example, mean one thing to the pedestrian and another to a car driver. 'Snow' has over thirty-five meanings to Eskimos, but very few to the average Westerner.

Our capacity to manipulate experience through concepts, ideas and symbols enables us to develop detachment and objectivity and yet we are still able to feel passionately according to circumstance and need. Writing about this feature of our human abilities Marris says;

'... this versatility is itself guided by an underlying integration of purpose, feeling and understanding, which enables us to choose, at any one moment, the most relevant mode of thinking, and to ignore irrelevant contradictions between one mode and another.' (P ix)

Meaning and Attachment

The in-built pre-disposition to create meaning and to become attached are twin forces which interact with our experience and according to Marris:-

'...form habits of feeling, behavioural strategies, perceptions of the nature of relationships and how to control them.'
and:-
'This development makes a sense of attachment crucial to the meaning of life, whether it is realised through a sexual bond, ties of kinship or even a symbolic figure.'

'A grown person can be self-sufficient, need not fear abandonment, and may have many purposes which do not relate directly to an attachment. (P ix)

But attachment itself :-
'is rooted in our emotional structures as the guarantor that these other activities and achievements will be worthwhile. Attachment is so central to our security in childhood that it becomes embedded, ineradicably, in the meaning of safety and reward for the rest of our lives.' (P ix)

Hence changes which disrupt the specific pattern of attachment upon which anyone depends, will disrupt their ability to experience life as meaningful, plunging them into grief, however rational these changes may seem from the point of view of someone with other attachments.

Chapter Ten

Types of Loss

Sudden Loss and Imperceptible Loss

There are some losses which are immediate in their impact - losing car keys, or losing a child in a supermarket. Others are imperceptible: losing one's strength in the ageing process or losing one's looks. These are examples of slow, inexorable loss. We react in a far more protracted way to such slow, long-term losses.

There are some crucial differences between sudden and long-term loss. In the case of an immediate loss, reactions are often related to very immediate needs. There is no time for preparation or anticipation, no rehearsal or practice in our coping mechanisms. It is not in our consciousness that we might have to face such a loss. We arrive in a situation and suddenly the news is given to us and we have to cope.

Imperceptible loss, however, is often subconsciously recognised. Long after it is over, we can go back and begin to recognise that even in the earliest days there was a dim sense of understanding, a slim recognition or acknowledgement at some level of our consciousness of what might unfold. Even if dismissed at the time, or acted against until the moment when recognition of the loss becomes inescapable, there are often hints and signals of what is to come.

'Misplacing'

People will often use terms to imply that they have not lost something, but simply *misplaced* it. Only later does the time come when, still unsure of its whereabouts, they finally recognise that it is lost.

Such strategies enable the article to become lost without our ever having to acknowledge responsibility, or our degree of attachment to the object.

Misplacing something is a means of denial. Indeed the object may turn out not to be lost after all. Many things do reappear, but not everything that we misplace is like this. We do actually lose some things. Rather than face it, or deal with the situation, we describe them to ourselves as 'misplaced'. Such psychological devices enable us to bear the prospect of not having something, in the belief that at some point we might have it again. Finally, though, we may have to give up the pretence and admit that which is gone is now lost irrevocably.

Our way of describing it in these terms helps us to escape the recognition and emotion of the immediate experience. We buy replacements and someone else says, 'Is that a new key-ring?' or 'I thought you'd lost that diary,' and we hear ourselves very casually say, 'Oh yes' or, 'Well, I had, so I bought a new one,' not realising our skill in being able to lose things without facing the consequences. And we use similar mechanisms in order to make bearable other, much more painful and deeply felt losses.

Joanne had been brought up in an orphanage with her sister. She had married and had a family. Her life on the surface had been successful, especially considering her start in life. However Joanne knew things differently on the inside of herself. She was still frightened and uncertain, still a person who knew the world to be uncertain and unpredictable. She was still someone who did not in any real way feel she 'belonged', so she could never feel that anyone truly cared about her - however much they said they did. Not surprisingly she tested all her relationships to the limit and beyond. In this way she had a stormy domestic life of constant dramas and scenes.

After a powerful experience, Joanne rediscovered many of her lost connections. She re-visited the old orphanage and found one of the ageing Sisters who brought her up. Together they talked of the horrors of the way children were treated. The Sister confirmed that much of what Joanne thought she had fantasised was all too true. Many of the abrupt decisions that were made and which affected her life in fundamental ways had indeed happened. For Joanne, her story, previously dismissed even by herself, as exaggerated and unreal, was beginning to be her own. She went, soon after, with her sister to the home of a relation and there had a meeting which added more to her story of lost connections. The encounter gave her the courage and the commitment to return to the land of her origin and to seek out the beginnings of her story.

Listening to Joanne when she returned was a moment of joy as she described the reawakening of all her lost family connections. The embrace and welcome with which she had been met affirmed that her lost 'belongingness' had a good foundation in reality. To all her 'tribe', as she described them, she had indeed been all but lost. Once they knew her to be alive she had a place at the hearth that was hers forever.

The profound effect of such acceptance upon Joanne's sense of herself as an individual, a woman and mother is still having repercussions. In part Joanne had lived a life constructed around managing the loss of what had been taken from her at such an early age and the subsequent absence of so many of those things ordinary children take for granted. The effects of loss runs throughout Joanne's story and will continue in new forms as she grows further into self-understanding.

Reactions to Loss

Loss often makes us sharply aware of fear, guilt or shame; of how we may have abused ourselves, others, or the situation; of how we must have failed. Loss can seem so arbitrary, so unwelcome and unbidden that we can be left believing that somehow we must have been responsible, that we must have been able to do more, or that we must deserve to suffer because somehow we must be in the wrong for this (whatever it is) to be happening to us. Sometimes, of course, these feelings are appropriately connected to the actual experience of the loss we are facing.

We may well act insensitively; we may live to regret our lack of consideration in the way we have treated others. We do look back on events and feel angry at the way we wanted to put off doing something constructive and useful. Instead, we were just too busy and therefore contributed to the worsening of the situation or event we did not want to happen. We can be negligent, delaying action whilst intending to ultimately put things right, until someone gets hurt or complains.

We do feel guilt when we have agreed to take up a commitment we then fail to honour. We do make agreements that we know we do not intend to fulfil, or cannot fulfil adequately given our other commitments. We do all these things - at least I know I do. When something unexpected happens - the situation turns sour, the complaint is made or the accident happens, then we can become paralysed with guilt, fear and shame.

But the real admission of failure and the genuine confrontation with our mistakes is a necessary part of growth and development. Fear, shame and guilt are all part of the spur to change and grow, but of themselves they can be paralysing and demoralising. Time and again we get locked into a sense of self-pity and reluctance to move on, because we use our mistakes to protect us from changing, or from learning what we need to see, claiming we are not worth the effort. We celebrate our failings, being only too willing to sing out our guilt to all those who will listen, never realising that doing so ensures that we remain precisely where we are.

We are then reminded of all that is left unfinished and we are thus made powerless to change any of it, because it is already too late to make any difference. We are left with the choice of either lingering over our mistakes or confronting our failures and learning the lesson that we have to admit and recognise. That gives us the opportunity to move on by taking responsibility for our part, exchanging blame for pain as we give conscious recognition to the discomfort our failings bring upon us.

Loss as a Relief

There are other losses, losses that are a relief, a great release: when we feel unburdened of the need for further effort. There is then a great sense of peace: it is all over. All the struggle, the pain, the uncertainty and grief is at an end and we may sink back into ourselves, a little ragged and dishevelled, but nonetheless relieved. There may be loose ends, small details to attend to, but the need for vigilance and foresight has gone.

This can be experienced as a feeling of retreat to safety and protection. We have survived. We have made it! We may feel this way for only a short time, or sometimes for longer periods, as the sense of relief holds us in a place beyond the usual realm of our daily life.

A near miss in a car, for example, can be sufficient to generate all these sensations, but it usually lasts only a short time. The conclusion to a long-standing conflict will often create that sense of surprise and even mild euphoria as we look back and realise we have suffered for such a long time, wondering how it was that we were able to cope in a way that went well beyond our expectations and our usual limits of endurance.

Coping Mechanisms

These are brief examples of the kinds of coping mechanisms that are at work when we lose something, especially when we are unprepared for the loss, or do not know how to admit that we have lost something.

Immobilisation.
This cannot be happening to me. We are unable to plan, reason, accept or understand what the loss means.

Minimisation.
We cope by pretending that the impact will be trivial, by denying it and making light of the loss.

Depression.
We withdraw, feeling useless, but here there are the beginnings of facing up to reality. However, new demands can cause immense frustration.

Bargaining.
Our expectations are reduced, but we use the loss as a bargaining chip to say, *This will give me the chance to do something else [that I've always wanted to do]*. The loss is avoided by searching for something else to take its place.

Acceptance.
At last we face up to the significance of what has taken place and our part in it, and begin to feel the release that ensues.

Chapter Eleven

Grief and the Trauma of Loss

Facing the implications of a major change, or a life threatening condition, interrupts our basic life processes; our capacity for thinking, feeling and willing, corresponding to the rational, emotional and active parts of our lives.

Thinking.
Our ability to think enables us to comprehend the world, ourselves and those around us. It is a truism that there is much that human beings do not understand. Great mysteries remain - death being one of the greatest. The sudden impact of a life threatening condition brings with it an all too forceful a reminder of just how much we do not know and how little we can think our way through an event that is literally beyond our comprehension.

Feeling.
When someone close to us is about to die, or we ourselves face death, our capacity to feel and love is grievously disturbed. We are sent into a turbulent mix of emotions, which may lead us into hysteria, panic or shock, as it reminds us of how unpredictable and in so many ways how out of our own control our emotional well-being is.

Acting.
When faced with events over which we have no control, we are brought face to face with the limits of our capacity to choose and to act. Whatever we do will not prevent what is happening. However hard we attempt to make a difference, things will be a certain way, a way we cannot change. Our influence is limited and with that recognition goes a sense of frustration and anger.

Interruption

Interruptions to these three processes produce the three characteristic emotions which constitute distress patterns. They cycle and weave their way through people's lives during the various stages of traumatic change and loss.

When our capacity for understanding (or thinking) is reduced, FEAR is produced.
When our ability to love and feel is weakened, we are sent into GRIEF
When our potential for action is decreased our frustration turns into ANGER.

The challenge of change for our understanding is to **take charge** of ourselves and to bring order and coherence once more into our lives. In relation to our ability to feel, the challenge is to **maintain and bring our relationships to an emotional close.** In the case of our will, it is to bring the anger under some management, so that we **complete those tasks** and activities we have time for and that matter to us.

Reactions to Interruption

Each of these three processes has its associated reactions, which may go to certain identifiable extremes.

Thinking.
If we take thinking first, the extreme reaction is to go into denial, where the individual continues to act as though nothing has changed and as though they are totally omnipotent, able to control everything that takes place. Such individuals are difficult to deal with, since any reminder of their mortality or their limitations may produce a harsh attack on the helper by way of reaction.

Alternatively, the response may be, not one of denial, but one of 'acting out'. This may take the form of attachment to compulsive rituals, or obsessive and unrealistic behaviour that, it is hoped, will keep the loss or impending threat at bay. Such acting out is a way of trying to forestall the inevitable. It can create great difficulty for helpers because whilst such behaviour may bring comfort and may even be necessary for a time, the ultimate emotional cost of managing such behaviour is often beyond anything that can be afforded.

Feeling.
When love is interrupted, an extreme reaction may take the form of withdrawal, of effectively saying; *Since you are going to leave me anyway, I will cast you aside first.* How often, in the final stages of life, is a patient left alone because their relatives can no longer bear to see them? Such withdrawal can be understood as a form of anticipated rejection, as a way of trying to cope with the inevitable loss of the individual.

Alternatively, reactions at the other extreme may take the form of *Since I know I must lose you, I must spend every moment possible with you before you go.* People begin to make clinging demands on one another and the dependency that may have been there in the past becomes far worse, making the relationship claustrophobic. It then becomes difficult for either party to make a satisfactory end to the relationship.

Willing.
When our will and the ability to choose are interrupted, the frustration and anger may be followed by periods of great depression. Energy to take on and complete any tasks may totally desert people. They may sink deeper and deeper into a sense of being a helpless victim. Whilst it is understandable that people will feel depressed at times,

such depression as this, which renders people totally passive and helplessly dependent on others, is pathological rather than helpful. This is not to say that people suffering should be *jollied* out of it - far from it. The sufferer is usually all too aware of just how passive and lifeless they are being. They simply cannot summon up the energy to do anything about it.

The opposite reaction uses the anger at the impending loss and turns it into oppression; taking out on others their fear and hurt at what they imagine is about to happen to themselves. It is not uncommon for helpers to be abused by families and friends when loved ones die, or to be blamed for not having done enough when in fact everything possible had been tried. Such oppressive behaviour is an example of people facing the reality of a situation that is outside their control and they cannot bear it. Someone must be blamed - it has to be someone's fault.

Individual Attitudes and the Process of Grief
The Journey to the End

Whatever style of response an individual presents initially, it is likely to change with time as they move through the stages that were first characterised by Elizabeth Kubler-Ross.

We can see that in the beginning the individual goes through a period of something approaching benumbing shock, which serves to hide the underlying fear that goes with one's mortality being brought into focus.

The period of **denial** helps to soften the blow by creating a period in which body and mind can mobilise their defences and resources for a response which will come later. The stage of **anger**, which is an expression of the impotent rage that one can influence so little in the face of what is taking place, will then give way to one of **sadness, of mourning and longing** for all that will not be and all that one thought would happen. This moves on to **bargaining**, of beginning to acknowledge and accept the possibility of something about to happen and an attempt to try to barter for a change in the situation by being willing to make some sacrifice in return for a release from the circumstances.

Gradually there is a move into **withdrawal,** where the individual concentrates more fully on what is happening to themselves. In the case of someone facing death through illness there is a deeper withdrawal into themselves as relatives and friends, except of the closest kind, start to become a pressure and a burden. In the final stages, the individual is likely to move towards an **acceptance** of their own mortality, a recognition that what will be will be, and that what will be will be manageable. This can then lead to the **peaceful victory over fear** that comes with the final moment of a gentle death.

The Importance of Individual Difference and Choice

Not everyone travels this journey either so succinctly or in such a linear fashion. For many people the journey is a halting, broken and discontinuous series of experiences that only the assistance of a skilled helper will help to integrate into a sense of significance and meaning. Many fail to complete the final stages of the journey, but many more do than do not. Many people can be helped to complete those last stages, having been given an important opportunity to seek meaning and understanding in the life that has been theirs, and been enabled to accomplish those final acts which matter so much, if they are to bring their lives to a satisfactory close.

Not everyone is able to take such responsibility for themselves, nor indeed can everyone be expected to. So we must look at the attitudes that people have when faced with the news of death.

We can distinguish four main types.

Those in Charge

There is a group of people who are ready to seek responsibility and manage the situation as effectively as they can. They form the group who seek to take charge of their own death.

Such individuals want to remain responsibly involved right from the beginning of any threat to their life, all the way to the final stages. They frequently have a strong internal belief in something and are able to take responsibility for what happens for the time remaining to them, even during periods of doubt, anguish and fear. They are often an inspiration to others and can help bring peace and resolution both to their own life and to those around them.

The Nervous Type

A second group is those who are nervous of taking such direct and open responsibility for what happens to them, but who will respond in this way if given a suitable opportunity.

For many there is the fear that they cannot cope with facing their own death. They may feel they are ill-prepared and unsure of what lies ahead, or what might be required of them, yet they may still wish to do what they can for themselves and for those around them. Such people are often an inspiration to others, because the reality of the situation that they face brings forth from them tremendous qualities that enable them to overcome the fear of being unable to cope. They may remind us of ourselves in that there was nothing in their prior history to predict such a brave, courageous and yet very human way of dealing with such a situation.

The Defended

A third group is those who are much more defensive, but who nevertheless will still respond well when confronted supportively.

Such people, like the previous group, have many more resources for responding to the situation than they often believe. They may require a firm challenge in order for them to take on the situation. If left without such a challenge, they will languish, unhappy in the knowledge that they could have done more, but somehow did not know how to begin to respond. Such people need help to surface their fears and concerns. They also need opportunities to work through them with support from those around so that their real strengths and talents can be released to take on the situation and move forward successfully.

The Refusers

The final group, however, is those who cling to their defences and take them to the grave. These are the people who do not want to know, who, for whatever reason, refuse to face what is happening and want to keep that position, from the very first hint that anything might be wrong, right through to the very final stages of life. At this point they may well make a sudden change, but for however long they hold to their refusal, it is their right.

It is unlikely that efforts by helpers to attempt to change such attitudes during the last stages of an individual's life will be of any real benefit. The question which must be asked is 'Who would benefit from these efforts anyway?' Such individuals are often vulnerable and know only too well what is happening to them, but for one reason or another they cannot manage to talk about it or deal with it openly. Nevertheless, in the final stages they may respond if they have been cared for patiently and not been made to feel guilty for the reactions they have had.

Chapter Twelve

Facing the Impact of Death

Facing Oneself

A life threatening illness, or a life challenging event, is likely to make an individual question their self-image, their view of themselves and their identity, making them ask 'Why me?' or 'What have I done to deserve this?'

The diagnosis of a serious or terminal disease can sometimes be taken by the individual receiving it as a mark that they are somehow being singled out and stigmatised for being imperfect, as though they have been chosen in some fated way. Such feelings often force the individual into a period of withdrawal and fear.

Whilst such responses are irrational, they are very natural and when individuals do take upon themselves the blame for what has happened helpers need to be patient at this stage. You will hear comments like *'This should not be happening to me,'* or *'This is not how I thought of myself as ending up'*.

Support and patient attention can make a great deal of difference at such a time. The reason behind such responses is that the individual's assumptions, their *world view,* is going through massive and unexpected change. Their identity will, for some time at least, become insecure. This may bring about fears of a lack of approval, or lack of the kind of support that has in the past been guaranteed. This is especially true of people dying of an illness which may carry social implications, such as HIV infection.

In such a case, for example, parents may have to confront losing a son or a daughter at a much earlier stage of life than they would have expected, and at the same time learn that their child is dying of an illness that is still little understood and greatly feared. On top of all that, they may well have to confront, perhaps for the first time, the recognition that their son or daughter is gay, lesbian or a drug user. Such difficulties cannot be over-estimated, nor how far they attack and undermine an individual's sense of their wholeness, reminding them of the fragility of their personal security. The following piece of writing is an extract from one person's experience of having to face the likelihood that they would have their life brought to an arbitrary close. Reading it, you can follow the mixture of feelings and emotions, the rational and the mental sides struggling to find an appropriate balance in a situation beyond the usual realms with which we are expected to cope.

When I was twenty six years old I very unwillingly began a journey. I had no awareness at the time of what I was doing or of where my road would take me. It took me eighteen months to find my way. What I should like to do is to share with you some of my experiences. When I first travelled down this road I went

alone, I had no choice, over the years I have re-traced my journey many times and shared part, or all of it, with several people. If you are able to come with me I don't know where the road will take you or what you will find when you reach the end.

For me this began when I learned that I had inherited a cardiac defect. It is a condition which was unrecognisable when I was a child. Today it can be diagnosed and treated in childhood. It is also, or it is supposed to be, a killer. This was to be the Consultant Cardiologist's dilemma; he had never seen anyone as old as me. Nobody lived that long. He was somewhat surprised to be confronted by a 5ft 6", 9 stone obviously ambulant patient. He was horrified when I advised him that I had kept horses all my life, had been a member of the Quorn Pony Club's Prince Philip Cup Team, played tennis for Nottinghamshire Schools, wasn't too bad at judo and had a young son. The problem was a deformed aorta; this restricts the circulation. Children born with this do not grow properly, their bottom halves, particularly their legs, deprived of blood never develop normally and most are wheel-chair bound from an early age.

In my case the veins round my rib cage had enlarged and the blood supply flowed down my back instead of down my front. He offered me two choices, certain death within four years or surgery with - because of my rather novel plumbing - very questionable results. At least he was honest and said he had no idea what to expect. Initially, I put up a very determined defence; I decided that I would have anything they liked except this. Most of the time I felt O.K. but the attacks which began during pregnancy were increasingly regular and incapacitating. My heart would race, I would become very dizzy and was in great pain. On one occasion I became incontinent. Towards the end of these attacks, which lasted anything between a few minutes to several hours, I was violently sick. I decided the problem was my stomach and I stuck to it. I stuck to it so firmly that I spent the next four months having a gastroscope, a barium meal and heaven only knows how many X-rays, all of which drew a blank.

Finally, I was left with no choice but to accept the diagnosis and all that went with it. I was offered a bed, I turned it down, it was nearly Christmas. I wasn't going to die at Christmas.

During the next twelve months the hospital sent for me five times. The first time the dog was 'ill', the second I was busy, the third I was going on holiday. The fourth time I really thought I would go. I went for a drink with some friends the lunchtime before and I remember nothing until the following night. I woke up the following day in my own bed too hungover and disgusted with myself to even bother phoning the hospital and explaining why I had not arrived.

My behaviour was so alien to me that I couldn't reconcile it. It was illogical, stupid and I was beginning to despise my inability to get it together. On top of this I had a seven year old son to care for and I was no use to either of us. The condition is hereditary and he would have to undergo the same surgery.

I began to see that I had during all this time been running an alternative script. I'd been practising dying or at least I had been trying to. Like a child who is afraid of the big waves I paddled around a bit then ran back to the shore. I could not seem get past my inability to imagine being dead. I could imagine going to theatre and not coming back alive. I could envisage the death bed scene, if I made it back and then died. I tried to tell myself that I was not indispensable, that my son was young he would forget me, but how would I know, I would be dead?

I couldn't go any further alone and everyone seemed more afraid than I. When I tried to talk about my fear I ended up comforting the person I was telling.

In early November I rang a colleague and said, 'If I don't find someone who is less afraid of my death than I am, I'm going to go completely mad'.

With her help, I finally found a way. I was beginning to make some sense of my life and of the fact that I might lose it and to realise that I could not risk losing my life until I could accept my death.

I began with the practical things, I made a will, spent a lot of time with my ex-husband discussing our son's future, decided on what sort of funeral I should have and for the first and only time in my life the house was tidy and I knew where everything was. I found that the prospect of losing my life at 27 years of age still didn't make any sense to me, but I came to realise that the 27 years I had lived were meaningful and could continue to be to the people I might leave behind. This led to the realization that I needed to find some way to make my death an expression of my life and of the way in which I would like those close to me to remember me.

I did not want their last memories of me to be filled with such pain and fear that they had to shut me out or worse; for their memories of my death to haunt them for the rest of their lives. I realised that I needed to leave them in a place where they could remember my life and death without pain and it became obvious to me that in their distress they would not be able to do this themselves. I would have to find the place and show them the way.

For me that meant killing all hope of living because whilst I hoped I would continue to fight and acceptance does not come from fighting. For someone like me who has always believed that I am responsible for my life and that all things are possible given sufficient application this was very difficult. Given the opportunity I would like to have been awake and supervising my own surgery. I recognised that I had to find a way of handing over responsibility to someone else, in fact the need to do this and gain some peace was becoming overwhelming, but I found it very hard to do. With no religious beliefs to fall back on I finally picked on the Surgeon; my life would literally be in his hands and I couldn't think of anywhere else to put down the burden. At last when I began yet again to go over the imaginary scenario I could tell myself to 'Stop. This wasn't my problem it was the Surgeon's' and I began to stop the ceaseless fretting.

One Thursday in mid-December I drove myself over to Blackpool Victoria Hospital and was admitted. My operation was to be the following Tuesday. I felt quite calm, I had checked and re-checked that I had done everything I needed to do. I had silently said my 'Good-byes' to everything and everybody and I was ready to die. I did not sleep at all that night. I paced up and down the ward, made coffee, smoked and played cards with the night staff. By Friday afternoon I was panic-stricken and then I realized that in a little over two weeks it would be Christmas and I hadn't done any Christmas shopping, there would be nothing of me there on Christmas Day. I phoned my would-be-weekend visitors and told them not to visit until Monday as I wanted some time on my own, I discharged myself from hospital promising to be back on Sunday and I drove home.

On Saturday I bought all my presents and a Christmas tree, for the first time ever I didn't buy a real one, I found the thought of it dropping its' needles as it died slowly in an empty house too painful to contemplate. During the evening I wrapped up the presents and put them under the tree. I didn't go to bed that night. In those days I had a coal fire and I sat all night in the dark with just the fire burning and the tree lights on. I thought back over all the Christmasses I could remember and I tried to look into the future. I imagined my seven year old son as an adult with a partner and children of his own and I wondered if they would remember me and if I would have any place in their lives. A part of me desperately wanted him to remember and make me live for them, another part of me wanted their lives to be too full and too happy for them to dwell on the past. But I did so want them just to give me a thought.

For me this was an enchanted night. I had somehow found a place that I have described since as a place beyond pain and beyond terror. It was a place in which I knew that everything was as it should be and where I felt free and at peace in a way I had never experienced before.

That place is still there for me and I can, and do, visit it whenever I wish or need to. It is a place without people and yet it is a place from which I feel able to reach out and touch others in a way which I can't do from any other place, a place where I feel in some way complete. I recall feeling that if I went outside, lay on the ground and concentrated hard I could dissolve into the earth and become a part of everything for eternity. The feeling remained with me when I returned to hospital on the Sunday and with it came a sense of another me, a me that was much older and much wiser than the everyday me, that could see and feel everything from a great distance and knew that whatever happened was meant to be.

In the last twenty four hours before surgery, I looked at everything for the last time. My last sunrise, last rain, the last time I would watch the evening news. I remember standing in a corridor clinging to a radiator with tears pouring down my face watching my last sunset.

I had quite a backlog of visitors who came to see me, some tried to cheer me up. They were the most difficult to be with, I didn't really want any of them, they were pulling me back and I didn't want to go. I found that I was alone in a way that I never have been before but have always been since. Not because I was or am lonely but because I had made this journey alone and at the end of it I had found a place where I could be at peace with myself.

I believe that I am very privileged to have made this journey, I am perhaps one of a small minority in that I was able to make the return journey. Sometimes I try to imagine what I would have been without it. I am only ever able to conclude that I would feel impoverished. It was without a doubt the most terrifying experience I have ever had. The journey seemed endless at the time and yet now, when I look down the road I travelled, it is comforting and familiar. When I visualise the place at the end of my journey I am sitting on the top of a cliff looking down into a valley. There are no people in the valley, just grass, trees, flowers and wild animals roaming free. The sun shines and there is a light breeze, just enough to ruffle my hair and move the long grass below. At the foot of the cliff there is a huge pool of dark water from which, reflected in the light that is life I believe for the first time I found and loved myself.
Liz Emmott

Life Stage

The age at which an individual is facing death, either their own or that of someone close to them, can make a huge difference to the way they react and how they may ultimately begin to be able to make sense of what is happening to them. Losing one's parent in later life is not usually experienced so seriously as losing a parent in one's teens, though obviously the loss of a parent is serious at any stage of life. The loss of a child by tragic accident to a young couple is likely to be experienced differently to that of the death of an adult son or daughter, though both losses are unbearably hard to face. Some losses serve to remind us of how suddenly we are no longer like those around us and we feel cut off, marked out and isolated

Facing death, like other major changes which single out individuals as being different from their peers, can be debilitating and isolating. They push those suffering further away from the human contact which may be the very thing needed to help them overcome the loss. Helpers need to be alert to this and offer support where necessary.

Mutual Support

Where others are undergoing similar trauma, there is the possibility of a sense of shared experience and the opportunity of finding mutual support. In recent years there has been a growth in the formation of self-help groups to enable people sharing the same experience find ways to manage their condition or difficulty. Self-help groups offer a new form of support for those not well catered for by conventional provision. From the foundation of Alcoholics Anonymous over thirty years ago (perhaps the model for all subsequent self-help groups), there are now organisations to share information, offer support and overcome the crippling isolation and fear associated with loss and other problems. Connecting people in need with such support groups can be a vital stage in the helping process. It may be an important first step on the road to recovery.

Not everyone, it should be remembered, will want to join a group, however much they might benefit from it, and such suggestions should be made tentatively. It is not unusual for such a suggestion to be taken as an indication that the helper is getting fed-up with the sufferer, or as a signal that the helper believes they should be *pulling their socks up and getting on with it*. Such suggestions need to be approached with care.

Separation and Loss

Whether it is contemplating the loss of something of our own - a limb, a relationship, or even our life - or whether it is the loss of someone close to us, we are vividly reminded of the extent of our own separateness and the need we have to find ways of standing alone.

Dependency relationships, which have meant close bonds, may make us feel unable to cope, or unwilling to face the future, as well as powerless to take our life in our own hands. Additionally, there will be a measure of personal grief to be felt over the loss we face.

There will be **fluctuating emotions of fear, grief and anger** as we move, with little control or direction, through a sea of feelings. The alteration of our sense of time and the difficult experience of having our future painted differently from any expectations we may have had, will further undermine our anchor points in life.

In addition, we also have to come to terms with facing the limitations of our personal influence. Life is no longer ours, no longer something we control and manage for ourselves. Life intrudes upon us, with the stark reminder that it too has its own contribution to make, irrespective of any interest or wish of our own. We simply have to live it out. The shock of the knowledge that faces a parent when they hear of the death of a child is an example of the future being rewritten in front of their eyes in ways that they would never have expected and would never have wished.

Unresolved Issues and 'Unfinished Business'

Whether the end may be marked by a person's death or the finishing of a relationship, even when loss is anticipated and to some degree expected, there may come with it the sense of having to confront and take responsibility for the unresolved issues that remain. At such times we are brought face to face with a sense of our own responsibility. Have we the courage to put things to rights, or shall we quietly let them subside and slip out of mind in the hope that they will go away? The pain of facing the past, dealing with issues and difficulties that lie there, and attempting to clear them, can appear too great a challenge at a difficult time. We may wish to withhold, in the hope that the difficulties will somehow magically cease to matter. Of course they do not.

Personal, unfinished business can get very much in the way of the final phases of any long-term relationship. It may well require great courage at a time of uncertainty to face a friend or relative with the issues that stand in the way and ask to have them dealt with. It can however bring about liberation, closeness and a deeper and more abiding trust.

One of the difficulties that can occur when people face loss of life, or loss of a partner, is that thanks to the well-meaning efforts of others they are discouraged from being honest with one another on the grounds of protecting the other party. This rarely succeeds. There are all too many examples where people have acted in what they thought were the best interests of another and withheld from them the truth of a situation. It can poison a relationship and make a lifetime of satisfactory closeness finally fail. Helping people surface unresolved issues and identify unfinished business, so that they can choose what to do about it, is an important contribution any helper can make.

Uncertainty About the Process

When an individual receives information which has life-threatening implications, the state of shock that immediately ensues is likely to make them unable to understand or be clear about the possibilities that lie ahead. Helpers need to pay attention to this and give the individual the time and space they may need to ask the many, many questions which will arise, and to go over and over what is known about the process involved as fully as possible. If this does not happen, it can leave the person feeling uncertain and isolated, believing everyone knows except themselves. Often they do not feel able to ask for the information they need.

As a result, there are many occasions where an individual simply allows themselves to be managed through a process they know little about, because they are too afraid to ask, or feel they have no right to demand information.

The more people know about what is likely to happen to them, the more they are able to contribute usefully to what takes place and the more they can then take charge of their own life and death.

Receiving the News of Death

The shock of receiving sudden, traumatic news, whether it concerns ourselves or someone close to us, frequently comes as a brutal interruption to the three major functions central to being human we looked at in a previous section: our capacities to feel, think, and use our will. When these three processes are simultaneously broken into by the massive interruption of an unexpected and unpredictable event, we are suddenly and overwhelmingly faced with the extent of our own powerlessness and inability either to understand, change or influence things.

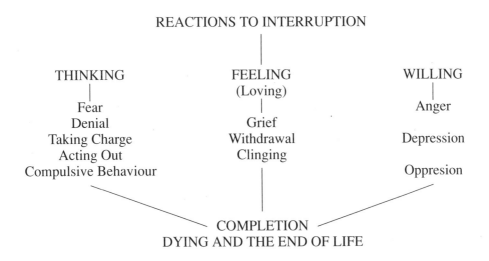

REACTIONS TO INTERRUPTION

THINKING   FEELING   WILLING

(Loving)

Fear   Anger

Denial   Grief

Taking Charge   Withdrawal   Depression

Acting Out   Clinging

Compulsive Behaviour   Oppresion

COMPLETION
DYING AND THE END OF LIFE

Figure 4

HUMAN CAPACITIES AND THE EFFECTS OF INTERRUPTION

We often revert to old, exaggerated patterns and styles of behaving rather than finding a new way through this difficult period. Such patterns may last for a while, or may be momentary, before the individual's turbulence subsides and they begin to find a way through the difficulties of coming to terms with an event that not only has immense significance in itself, but also puts them in touch with their own impotence and limitations. Some of the many issues that are raised by such intrusions are dealt with in this section.

Responding to the News of Death
First and false reactions

The ways in which human processes are interrupted by dramatic news have already been outlined, this section looks at the way individuals demonstrate their response to such news and the different forms this may take. Some of the forms are a mixture of those outlined below. Sometimes they cycle quickly from one response to another before finally settling on a characteristic style of responding.

However, there is a range of ways individuals rely upon to cope with receiving traumatic news. They may, for instance, go through *panic, shock, rage, frustration, disbelief and denial, blaming others, exaggerating their response, dramatising the situation, or even hysteria.* They may try to *resort to humour* and make jokes. They may attempt to draw the person who brings the news into some kind of collusive agreement to avoid dealing with the realities of the situation. They may attempt to *ramble on and on* as a way of overcoming the resistance to the news that the helper has to bring. They may try to *take over* the situation and put the helper at ease with the pretence at acceptance. There may be *false heroism*, or its opposite - *collapse and confusion.*

Underlying Fear

We can compress all these various styles of response into three distinct styles. Underlying all of them is **fear.** For some, the event that is about to occur is so painful to contemplate that they cannot get to it soon enough. They may even wish to end their own life rather than wait until the end comes about in the natural order of things. We must remember that **genuine acceptance is not 'giving in' or 'giving up'**, but a stage of growth into new experiences that can only take place after an individual has had time to incorporate into their psyche the trauma and difficulty, the pain and the humiliation that goes with the sudden interruption to one's life expectations. The three styles of response are outlined below.

Forms of Collapse

Four main types of collapse can be identified.

The first is where an individual simply gives up. Once the diagnosis is given, or the situation outlined, the individual takes no further part in attempting to influence it in any useful or important way.

The second is that of false acceptance. The individual quite sensitively, and apparently quite realistically, cooperates and accepts the diagnosis of the situation. For a long time they may be an ideal patient, and a model to others who are going through the same kind of difficulty.

Such false acceptance, however, has a toll that will inevitably appear at some point in the future. False acceptance often cripples people when they finally begin to realise their own limitations and the extent of their own suppressed anger and frustration. It can produce even more difficulties now that their response to their condition has become a role that everyone expects them to keep on playing.

Much easier to deal with are the **third and fourth kind of individuals who respond with confusion,** questioning that this must somehow be a mistake. The confused response is an understandable one and may only last for a short time, as part of the initial stages of their reaction to the situation.

It may however become a prolonged state of uncertainty and insecurity, where the individual simply will not and cannot find ways to make sense of the situation that now exists. The individual who challenges their situation as being somehow mistaken and waits for a re-definition, or a re-diagnosis that gives more hope, can also lay themselves open to long-term suffering by removing themselves from the possibility of any help whilst they deny what is taking place.

Forms of Rejection

We can identify three main forms of rejection - ways a person refuses to deal with the situation.

The first is **rejection that comes out of anger and blame.** The individual looks for someone they can make responsible for what happens and accountable for what is going to take place. This is simply a way of displacing their fear and concern at what is happening to them. It is not at all unusual for such individuals to embark on great crusades, attempting to right minute wrongs that they believe have been done to them at this stage, all as a method of keeping their energy and attention away from what is actually happening to them.

Secondly, and similarly, there is the individual who responds to the initial diagnosis with the **courage of heroism.** It is important to be aware that they may be operating out of an unrealistic sense of their own capacities.

Thirdly, there is the individual who moves into a position of **straight denial.** They will not talk about it, they do not want to know about it and they simply refuse to deal with it.

Forms of Avoidance

There are three principal ways in which individuals respond to a situation by avoiding it.

There will often be some attempt at involving the helper and others in some form of **collusion**, to minimise or even deny what is happening. An alternative is to **take the situation over** and manage it oneself, as if one were in charge of it.

Straight panic and hysteria sometimes surface and can last longer than many people imagine. It may be in the form of periodic outbursts that may bring some helpful release, but they may bring about no more than wild emotional excess.

Finally, **displacement** - the pushing away, either of the news, the consequences, or the situation from oneself - not necessarily onto someone else, but simply displacing a full sense of what is about to happen away from oneself, leaving oneself free to pretend life is other than it really is.

The Return of Death

Death was a precious, central experience in all ancient cultures and civilisations. It stood as a majestic, colossal and unknown experience: the centre around which all life was organised. Time, ceremony and elaborate ritual were all devoted to the experience of death.

It is only in our own time that we have responded to death with denial, disengagement and indifference. We have put it beyond the bounds of discourse. We have isolated it in an attempt to defeat it, but it has returned with fierce vengeance. The reaction that diseases such as AIDS provoke clearly displays how powerless and impotent we are to meet death, let alone respond to it. We have spent too much of our time pretending that it will not affect us, that it will not enter our lives and it will not be acknowledged by ourselves.

Death is with us once more. Death is the key to life. Only by accepting the finiteness of our individual lives can we begin to change and to discover our inner resources. The denial of death seduces us into leading empty, purposeless lives, since when we live as though we cannot, or will not, change we act as though we will go on forever. By freezing time so that our role stays the same, by fighting to keep our world changeless, it becomes all too easy to postpone doing the things we know we must do.

When we live life in expectation of tomorrow, or in remembrance of yesterday, we fail to live in the present, and each living moment and its potential is lost. Fully understanding that each day could be our last means that we have to take the moment to act, to grow and move towards being who we really are and drop the fears and concerns which hold us back.

There is an urgency then, to commit ourselves to being all that we can be. But we struggle to keep away that moment of committal, because it means giving up everything that is not truly ourselves. Many of us are afraid that there will be nothing inside ourselves to sustain us and that without those external confirmations of ourselves there will only be emptiness in our lives.

Doubt

Self-doubt keeps us from trusting ourselves enough to let go and discover the potential within us. We can only realise that potential if we give up trying to be someone other than who we really are. We have to give up concern for approval, for external confirmation of our significance and importance, and instead shift our awareness to considering what we are in relation to what we know. We have to reassess our beliefs to make them consistent with our personal values. Nothing is simpler and nothing is more arduous.

The Need to Embrace Death as the 'Ally'

How do we find the strength to reject those external definitions that tell us who we should be? Through facing and accepting death, not as an idea, not as something that will one day happen to us, to be ignored for the time being, but rather as a constant reality.

It is death that shows us the way to live our life fully. When we know and understand that our time on earth is limited and that we have no way of knowing

94

when it will be over, then we can begin to live each day to the full. We have to act now - there may not be a tomorrow - to take one step at a time towards the realisation of our potential.

When this begins to happen life takes on new significance. It becomes possible to find in ourselves courage, strength, compassion and love that we were never aware of.

Awareness of death is the key to our own growth and development.

Section II
Recommended Reading

Bandler R & Grinder J   *Reframing: Neuro-Linguistic Programming and the Transformation of Meaning.*
Real People Press   1982

Dilts, R   *Beliefs: Pathways To Health And Wellbeing*
Real People Press   1990

Hill, S   *In The Springtime Of The Year*
Penguin Books   1989

Lewis, C S   *A Grief Observed*
Faber and Faber   1990

Littlewood, J   *Aspects Of Grief*
Routledge   1993

Marris, P   *Loss And Change*
Routledge and Kegan Paul   1986

Scott Peck F   *The Road Less Travelled*
Arrow   1978

Tatelbaum, J   *The Courage To Grieve*
Cedar   1990

Whitaker, A (Ed.)   *All In The End Is Harvest*
Darton Longman & Todd   1984

Wilber, K & T   *Grace And Grit*
Gill & MacMillan   1992

Worden, W   *Grief Counselling And Grief Therapy*
Springer, New York   1982

Vaughan, F   *The Inward Arc*
Shambala   1986 (OP)

Section III
The Role and Tasks of the Helper
in Helping People Change

Anyone can listen to the wise but the true helper will listen to anybody they happen to meet. Because the person they meet next might have the very thing most needed for the next step on their own journey. But they won't notice that, or be aware of it and they will never see that if they are too busy trying to be *helpful*.

Be helpful by being still and letting the person unfold before you.

We need to learn to die in order that we can begin to learn to live. Growing to be who we truly are may sometimes demand of us that we die to the life chosen for us by society; each step of growth involves throwing off more of the shackles which restrain us. In order to grow, we must continuously die and be reborn, in much the same way a caterpillar becomes a butterfly.

Our final opportunity for growth comes only when we are at death's doorstep, but we do not have to wait until then. By understanding the growth and life-enhancing properties of dying, we can learn to die and grow at any point we choose.

The qualities that predict our being able to deal effectively with our death are the same qualities that distinguish us at any stage in life.

Chapter Thirteen

The Relationship Formed in Crisis

The Helper as an Agent of Change

As we have already discovered, we live in times of unprecedented change: social, political, organisational, economical and personal. Solutions to dilemmas and difficulties familiar to previous generations are being swept away. Social certainties and political realities are changing at astonishing speed because organisations are going through a process of continuous transformation that began in the 70's and which shows no signs of slowing down. We are now living in a *global village,* a term first used by Marshall McLuhan in the 60's, which seemed preposterous at the time, but which, thanks to the speed and sophistication of media communications, has become commonplace. The *global crisis* is something no-one on the planet can not have heard about.

And yet there is another side to all this. Change is always with us. There have always been times when people have needed a listening ear to help them through their storms and trials. Some changes are unchanging too. Bereavement and loss are part of the human condition. We cannot be on the planet without enduring our fair measure of suffering.

Our attitudes to the human situation shift. How we look upon what happens to us, what meaning we bring to our experience and what significance we find within it, affects fundamentally how we respond to what is happening to us. The context of our lives and the social values which surround us form the backdrop to our individual reactions and responses. Helpers need to remember this every bit as much as the need to respond to the particular individual.

Helping people recover some measure of coherence, or identify some meaning to what may appear as unique and isolating experiences can be crucial aspects of the healing process. However much the release of distress and the discharge of pain and hurt are vital ingredients in the process of letting-go of loss, so too is placing the events themselves within a developing framework of our understanding of life, something all too many people lack.

The absence of understanding, of significance, of having no inner world of meaning, or no vantage point from which to weigh the seriousness of events, leaves individuals prey to fantasies of the most debilitating kind and to fears that they are somehow *not normal,* not like other people.

In societies which still have rituals and rites of passage to mark significant transitions - periods of mourning for example - however isolated in her grief the widow may be, she is not isolated from her neighbours and community. All recognise the process in which she moves through her day.

In societies like ours no such rites hold sway. Individuals pass through all manner of upheavals that remain unmarked and unremarked. Platitudes and clichés replace real contact and fear of coming too close to another in pain, of finding the depth and extent of our wounds, keep the well-meaning helper in the role of patronising comforter or diffident supporter.

The *'There, there'* brand of concern or the *'Well, it will all be alright one day'* approach leaves the sufferer with no place to go. Feeling bad for feeling bad to start with, they only feel worse for having had it recognised and dismissed, or discounted so easily. Or they feel the anger, so necessary a part of the grieving process and then the guilt for feeling that too. Either way, they remain stuck in their individual well of pain and loneliness, unless they find a place or a person able to be with them in their pain; someone who is not seeking to make it better or to change it, but who will let them be and let them be 'in' their pain.

So often it is the struggle to keep up appearances, the determination to 'not let it show' that consumes vast amounts of energy. In the end, the pain of grief has to be faced and lived through and the need for the safety of another's presence is more important than all the techniques and skills in the world.

The art of the helper is learning to be there, as fully present as possible, freely open to allow the client to be, trusting to them and their own process to bring about the shifts which will encourage movement and change - however small - of a genuine kind. Attempts to jolly clients into change or to over-challenge them into tackling issues rarely work unless the counsellor is free of investment in the client **having** to change.

Building a Relationship in Crisis

Situations that confront helpers with a painful sense of how difficult it is to build a relationship with, or give comfort to, a stranger include responding to someone in crisis, approaching someone suffering the shock of initial grief or bereavement, speaking to a relative or loved-one of someone who has been injured or killed in an accident.

- **How do you know what to do?**

- **How can you decide what is wanted?**

We all know from experience how easy it is to say the wrong thing, quite by accident, or to have the grieving person misunderstand our best efforts. In addition, some people may respond to receiving difficult news by lashing out at those closest to hand.

There are those people who do not perceive themselves as needing help or wanting it. There are others who are initially passive and will appear to cope well, making life especially easy for the helper, because they don't make any fuss. And there are those who want to kick out at the unfairness and arbitrariness of what they have to deal with.

The helper cannot know in advance just who they are going to meet or what reaction they are going to face. Such situations are often unpredictable and are far from easy to handle. They present the helper with the challenge of maintaining a firm sense of offering the best help they can and this may not be enough. It may not be understood, but it is worthy of respect. If you do all you know how, there is no more that can be asked of you.

Helpers are fallible and human too. Often the willingness to be there and sit with someone is a far more telling example of care than empty words or false reassurance. Simply to say 'I can be here beside you, but I have no words for what is happening,' can give someone the space to feel their pain yet supported in doing so by another's presence.

There are two initial tasks facing the helper at such critical times:

- **Finding a point of entry**

- **Establishing rapport at a difficult time**

Finding a Point of Entry

The person in crisis may be unpredictable in mood, difficult to reach, or over-reliant on false hopes. The helper has to listen carefully to the cues (which may be all too few) in order to establish a sense of where the person is. The helper must be willing to try several strategies - blustering cheerfulness can work with some people, but it is not helpful to a good many others. Finding ways to help the other person respond may be extremely taxing.

Establishing 'rapport' at a critical time

The term *rapport* is used to point out the importance of developing the relationship once some contact has been made. Relationships that begin as a result of a crisis, for example a nurse speaking to a parent about the loss of their child, give no time for preliminaries. Yet too abrupt an approach will only add to the shock and bewilderment. There is no right way of going about it, no approach which is guaranteed to work. The helper's sensitivities have to be acutely at work in order to identify and build upon where the other person is and to take the conversation at their pace.

Strategies to Help Someone in Change

Since the mover will not have their usual creativity and flexibility on call because of the stress involved in working through the change or transition, helpers can remind them of simple ways to cope more effectively. Not all suggestions will fit all cases, but these are some of the most easily adopted ways of managing the experience of over-exposure to change.

Filtering

Invite a person to select out the essential from the unessential bits of their world, those that require their attention, rather than their remaining stuck with an apparently unmanageable jumble.

Queuing

Help them prioritise the most essential tasks and identify the next step in one area they feel able to tackle. Helping them realise a useful improvement to a minor issue is better than a brave failure at a more significant one. In other words, *work for guaranteed results to build up confidence.*

Approximating

Suggest reducing standards of performance temporarily, to gain some slack for other things. Rather than not doing a task, offer a minimum standard so that it is completed and is not one more job stacked up to face later.

Withdrawal

Suggest leaving the situation for a time to gain a breathing space, then look at it from a different angle. Do not be too serious, but on the other hand, do not run away either. Withdrawal means choosing to move away from the situation for a time rather than avoiding it altogether.

The Importance of Listening

'A Good Listening is Soothing to the Heart.'

The value and importance of listening, of really hearing someone else by offering time, space and attention cannot be overestimated. In sharing our story with another, if they really listen, something will move. Change will happen of itself. The more fully we are listened to, the more we are able to move at our own pace.

Helping someone tell their story is the first and most vital part in helping. Through sharing their story, perhaps over many occasions, the individual begins to find pattern and coherence within their jumbled impressions and recollections. Gradually a sense of order and understanding will begin to emerge. Slowly, the individual begins to sense the place they have reached, or begins to gain a clearer idea of how far the situation has developed. Through such sharing, the individual

101

starts to develop an insight into their circumstances, or begins to recognise that they are managing a situation of high uncertainty with a real element of pain and distress.

It may be that there is more work to be done. Solutions may be out of the question. What solution is there, for example, for the mother whose child has been killed in a road accident? Listening may then be the most important way to help. Simply *being with* someone in their grief may be the most difficult challenge for the helper, but the most vital need for the sufferer who does not have to be alone with their pain, though they are, in an important respect, alone *in* their pain.

Experiencing Crisis

One of the difficulties for individuals receiving potentially threatening news is the fear of what they may hear and of having their worst fears confirmed. Waiting to be told potentially difficult news creates a vacuum in which people create fantasies, often imagining things to be far more difficult than in fact turns out to be the case. It is fears such as these, every bit as much as the actual facts of the situation, that begin to govern their reactions. It is essential for helpers to be aware of this dimension so that they will allow the person time and space to acknowledge their fears, begin to manage them and not be ruled by them.

Making Things Worse

Even less challenging news will generate fears and fantasies, leaving the individual unable to react capably to the news itself. They may then pass through a period of doubt about what the truth is. They may, in some cases, actually seek to make the situation worse than it is because then it would meet the expectations and fantasies they have generated for themselves. Such difficulties in hearing troubling news can make even the most considerate and sensitive helper's job difficult, or even impossible.

Pacing the News and Information

Helpers must make every effort to consider the person they are helping and to offer the news at a pace and in a way which suits them. They must do all in their power to ensure that the timing of the news is such that it gives the individual the best opportunity to manage themselves and the situation as best they can. Nevertheless, there is nothing a helper can do when faced with someone who will not respond, cooperate or take on the news.

There are those people who, in anticipation of hearing the worst, rush into begging for it, demanding that they are told as quickly as possible. Rarely do they cope with the news when it comes. Conversely there are those who passively sit and wait, asking nothing, until they are told.

These reactions can be seen as examples of the inability to know how to cope that is precisely what makes the situation difficult for both helper and client.

The client is in a situation that is highly unusual. The helper, however familiar with giving such news, must take into account the circumstances of the individual in front of them. Yet they may actually know nothing of those circumstances. This makes the whole enterprise uncertain.

Providing only the minimal information that the client can take in and leaving space and time for further conversation and follow-up are essential opportunities helpers must offer.

Working with feelings

Our culture discourages the freedom to feel openly and strongly, both positively and negatively. Unless helpers have worked through some of the oppressive restrictions and conditioning around the expression of feelings they are unlikely to be at ease in working with intense feelings in others.

The expression of some intense feelings may require encouragement and assistance to *act into* the feeling. It may well require agitated movement, hitting cushions and so on - feeling lies within the body and freeing the body is one way into encouraging the process of letting go.

All this may mean the display has a dramatic and artificial quality about it - in the beginning. It may also appear frightening to an unskilled observer or helper. **Working with intense feelings requires care and skill.** Feelings have no urge to immortality. When the freedom is given (not pushed for or demanded) to feel deeply and fully, whilst powerful and perhaps disturbing to begin with, the emotions will find their own dynamic of expression and ebbing away. Anger often gives way to tears; crying may lead to fury before a slowing down which may well be followed by a deep silence, indicating a period of re-evaluation that is best left respected by the helper rather than explored with a *helpful question*. This is what is meant by trusting the client and the process.

The client will often value the silent space to allow things to reshape themselves within their inner world. They do not need to give instant reports on the new landscape, or break off to reassure you they are *getting back to the room or moving out of it*.

Often it is the invitation to say more, to frame a thought, describe a memory, or enter more fully into a feeling which brings about release and movement. The gentleness of a delicate enquiry *How is it now?*, *Where did you go just then?* can be all that is required to provide the necessary encouragement for the process to move on.

Allowing the client to be free to feel is the intention, to let go of the need to stay in control or be seen to be 'over it'.

Moving On

But the freedom which arises as the feelings subside has to be managed and integrated. There will be many bouts of feelings to express in facing the loss of a deep relationship. There will be the stage when the client is tired of feeling, especially when the feeling is so painfully familiar; loneliness, emptiness, desolation and that sense that there will never be a consolation for this loss. It may well be a lonely time for the helper too. A time for recognising that there is nothing to be done to help, except to be there whilst this phase is endured.

Each session through such a phase, however, needs to be managed and the client brought back to the present reality. *Switching attention,* as it is known, is an important skill in re-orientating the client back to the world surrounding them.

This may take the form of inviting them to talk a little about the immediate tasks ahead; it may be to get them to focus, quite literally, on the details of some aspect of the room (to move them away from their feelings and into thinking). Such attention switching begins to give the client confidence that the feelings that so often threaten to overwhelm them can, in actual fact, be managed by them.

As the client begins to realise that a period of turbulent release can be brought under their management at the close of a session, an important move can take place. There will be a new understanding that there is a space for them to deal with feelings and discharge them in safety, so lessening the risk of them 'leaking out' inappropriately elsewhere.

Over-Investment

This is an important issue which should be thoroughly worked with in training and in supervision in order to free the helper to work more effectively for the client's benefit. Even where that has happened there will nevertheless be occasions when a situation or an issue a client is working through 'triggers' the helper's own 'material.' A skilled helper, however, can recognise this process very often. They will also recognise their own intrusion into the client's process and have some level of disquiet about the responses they offer which they will take to supervision. None of us are free of our own issues, recognising them and managing them is crucial when helping people change.

Chapter Fourteen

Change and Transitions:
Tasks and Stages

Tasks of Change and Transition

To acknowledge the reality and impact of the event
The mover must be enabled to face up to and recognise the change with a realistic sense of its importance and influence. This may take some considerable time.

Experience the accompanying feelings
Major change brings about emotional turbulence as well as potential for growth. Failure to work through the feelings associated with a significant change may lead to blocks in development later.

Make adjustment to the change and transition
Change also challenges the individual's understanding of themselves, the world, their place and the contribution they can make. Opportunities to reconsider and evaluate the impact of change are important factors in enabling an individual to grow in personal awareness and self-understanding.

Put emotional energy into the emerging situation
Some changes are emotionally demanding and draining, leaving the mover, for a time, unwilling to look outside the immediate situation or help themselves move on. Periods of recuperation, gathering energy and so on can become a habit leading to passivity, if left unchallenged for too long.

Major Conditions for Effective Personal Change
Conviction and Commitment

The first step in any successful attempt to bring about change is the **recognition of the need for change.** The person making the change has to be both convinced and committed to change within themselves. Without such commitment there may be attempts but there will never be success. It may take a good deal longer to obtain a genuine commitment for change than many helpers realise. **Commitment is harder to obtain than conviction.** People may be convinced of the need to change all kinds of things about themselves, but they are not necessarily committed enough to do anything about it.

The Need for Risk and Anxiety

There must be a sufficient level of turbulence or anxiety to make the risk of experimenting seem worthwhile. If it all seems too easy, it may be that something else needs to be changed.

Safety and Support

There must be enough trust in the relationship to explore and test out the possibilities of any proposed change and enough reward to make it worthwhile. People may be able to do things with a counsellor or even on their own, but not feel safe in the situation where it actually matters. Helping to create the safety where it matters may be a long-term process. It usually means creating a security zone within the client's own sense of themselves, an internal resource state that will give enough confidence for the person to tackle the real-life situation successfully.

A Real Meeting

Bringing about change has got to matter, not only to the client, but to the helper too. To the client it may be that the change is what has to matter, to the helper it is being effective in helping someone else accomplish a realistic change. If the helper is half-hearted about helping, then the client won't even be half-hearted.

Rehearsal

It helps most people to have a sense of what they are in for; how things might work and what might happen. This however is different from giving lectures, or holding someone's hand and doing it for them. It's more like offering a few clues at a sensitive point. The client can then build their own maps.

Experimentation

Talking about it won't do it. In the end the client has, where possible, to try out any new programme or behaviour in a live situation; a situation, as far as possible, where mistakes can be managed safely and appropriately, before trying it in the most challenging of circumstances. Doing so minimises the possibility of the client attempting the most difficult of examples at the outset, or tackling the most serious of issues at the first attempt. **Graded practice is essential. All of us have failed enough times. We don't need to keep practising that one!** The helper must seek ways to help the client build on success, however small.

Reflection

Now I can do it, is only one element in the successful resolution of a piece of change work. As the client gets closer to moving on, they need to develop the habit of reflection *'What does this all tell me about myself?'* *'How does this affect the image I have of myself?'* and *'What impact will this have on my other relationships?'*

Transfer

It won't work without practice. Helping people find times and places to practice what they are learning and to consider how to transfer such learning from one situation to another helps integrate change.

Beliefs Surrounding Change

It is useful and worthwhile for the helper to be aware of certain beliefs surrounding change:-

*   People can do it.

*   You don't always have to know why someone can't do something in order to help them learn how to do something.

*   The client can always identify people who can do what they want to do, who can be used as a base for modelling what they would like to accomplish.

*   People have more resources than they think.

*   People can make the best choice and if they can't, you certainly can't do it for them.

*   Some people find the idea of change and personal responsibility very threatening.

*   The ability to change is influenced by age, class, ethnic origin and so on, but it is not controlled by them.

*   Powerlessness is a self-generating spiral, creating meaninglessness, depression, leading to a sense of pointlessness.

*   You can't have anything you want, simply because you can always decide on things which are irrational and you can always sabotage yourself.

*   However, most people can have what they want, the problem is they don't know how to get it.

*   It is not that the world does not offer people most of what they would like, it is that they haven't got useful ways of knowing how to go about getting it .

Stages of Change and Transition

The following framework describes the key points of each of the main stages that connect widely differing change events. It is drawn from a range of sources and is largely concerned with the typical or predictable changes of day-to-day life: changing job or location, moving house, leaving a relationship. It helps explain the overall features of important changes and will often be useful in thinking through the effects of traumatic change.

There are two aspects to this framework, that of the 'mover' and that of the 'helper'. They are described side by side to enable the reader to gain greater insight into the two different perspectives and the stages and tasks involved in each.

Reaction Cycle for the 'Mover'

Not everyone passes through these stages in a straightforward manner, nor do individuals spend equal amounts of time within each stage. Individual progress is typically erratic, with periods of progress, punctuated by regression and occasional periods of feeling stuck. Although the reaction cycle given below must only be thought of as a general guide, it can be useful in a wide variety of situations.

I Immobilisation

This is a phase of *'It cannot be happening to me'*. The event is either so unexpected or so grave in its implications that the individual rejects the possibility of it happening at all. This is a stage of denial and can be seen as a necessary breathing space whilst the person mobilises their internal resources to cope with the impending change. Some people refuse to move beyond this stage. This is the period when it may well be plain to everyone else that things cannot go on the way they are and everyone has recognised the gathering forces of change, but the actual mover is still oblivious to it all.

II Minimisation and Depression

There is often a following period of making little of the event, making light of the situation generally, or of

The Helper's Stages and Tasks

Despite having the best of intentions, it is all too easy for helpers to bring the mover to a temporary halt by an over-hasty challenge or an over-supportive response. Challenge and support are both necessary and important facets of the helper's task, but identifying which is required and when it is needed is by no means simple. This section lists a series of pointers for the helper to bear in mind when working with someone moving through a transition.

I Pre-awareness:
Careful Observation

Resist all temptation to point out just how hard the mover is likely to fall. Do not give way to the temptation to say 'I told you so', when they have fallen. Gather information. Watch how the person operates, so that you can help them learn how they get themselves into such situations, in order that they can develop early warning systems of their own for future use.

If the person refuses to move beyond this stage, that is their right, and the helper will gain nothing by trying to force movement - even with the best intentions.

II Present Awareness:
Patience and Support

The mover may be hinting at their readiness to be helped but actually

Reaction Cycle for the 'Mover'

reducing the full implications of the prospect ahead. This is a time when people often attempt, unrealistically, to see the virtue in the inevitable.

At this stage, events gather together and change becomes inevitable. The deadline for the job application, or for handing in the piece of work cannot be denied any longer, but the mover is still not ready to act. This is the stage of reluctant recognition that the issue will not go away, though the mover may wish it would. In a positive change this would be the stage where someone starts to comb the paper looking for job advertisements, even though they have not yet decided that they definitely want a new job.

The full impact of an event is often signalled by a sense of depression and helplessness, if not outright hopelessness. False comfort is of no real help at this point. Depression signals the recognition that the individual is actually starting to face the situation and is about to begin to tackle it.

The realisation that all efforts so far have done nothing to forestall the inevitable is a necessary and depressing pre-condition for any forward movement. This may be a long-lasting phase that tries the patience of those intimately involved, because they too are likely to feel inadequate or feel that the whole thing has lasted *'too long'*.

III Bargaining

Bargaining, whilst unrealistic, is nevertheless a real sign of willingness to face things. The stage of saying *'If only ... then everything would be*

The Helper's Stages and Tasks

resist that help if offered. Their investment in the outcome is not yet sufficiently strong to be tested with serious challenge. Things may have to get worse before they can get better.

Helpers need to treat this phase with caution. Do not explode the bubble - it is all part of trying to cope. It shows signs of acknowledgement, however distorted.

Suggestions to 'pull yourself together' are all too easy to make, but they are of no use, since the mover will already be doing the best they can. Helpers must recognise such frustration as their own and keep it to themselves. Neither is it helpful to tell the mover that 'everything will be alright' or to give false platitudes or reassurance. It will not be helpful to exhort them to 'accept the inevitable' or 'to put up with it.'

The helper can be of greatest help by being there with the mover, trusting the process of the mover and supporting them in what may be a dark, depressing stage.

III Initial Engagement: Gentle Probing

This is the time when the helper can afford to become a little more active, probing the mover's uncertainties and

Reaction Cycle for the 'Mover'

alright' is a beginning of mobilising efforts to tackle things and suggests the return of the energy needed to make real progress. Now the helper can engage the individual in planning and deciding what strategy to implement. There may be some unrealistic expectations. Job seekers, for example, often apply for far too many jobs for which they are unqualified or unsuitable, or else think of trying careers for which they have no skill or preparation. But energy is now returning.

This is the stage where the mover shows at least minimal efforts at a response. It is often a time of half-hearted and unrealistic levels of commitment. It is the stage at which the mover wishes not to become over-invested in case the whole enterprise fails. It is still possible to withdraw gracefully and pretend it all doesn't really matter. Minimising one's chances or expectations is a feature of this stage. Students, for example, who will go on to do extremely well, will often say that they are not sure how they got on with an exam. This is a way of hedging one's bets.

The Helper's Stages and Tasks

gently confronting any exaggerated claims with light observations. This is not the moment to burst the bubble either, however beneficial you may believe it will be in the long run. It is far better to allow the mover to test out their own enthusiasm, or their growing suspicions that all may not be well.

IV Acceptance

A more realistic level of recognition is finally required. A certain degree of commitment must be declared if the mover is to make something of the opportunity or challenge ahead. Coming to terms with the actual conditions of, say, a new job, may mean dropping some of the grand schemes the mover has been talking about. This is a phase in which realism

IV Acknowledgement: Serious Exploration

Now is the time that enough experience and commitment have been mobilised for the mover to have concrete issues to face up to and work with. Serious exploration and open-ended questioning which leave options on the table to think about further are important. This is not the time to seek to offer some supposed

---

Reaction Cycle for the 'Mover'

begins to enter the picture.

Acceptance is not necessarily embraced positively. It is not always a recognition that the worst is over. Acceptance means facing up to the full implications and impact of the event.

Now there is a readiness to assess the full measure of what has happened. Now, too, a perspective and a timescale from which to view events becomes available to the mover. No longer is the event so immediate or so central.

This may be the long period of enduring the day-to-day reality of what it means to be alone, for example, after the drama of separation or divorce.

V Search for Meaning

Gradually the transition becomes part of the overall pattern of life. It is still important but no longer a pre-occupation. Other dimensions of life press for attention, after having been neglected. The mover must begin to adjust to the implications of the situation that are now beginning to appear explicit.

This is the period when the event is beginning to be placed in the context of the growing themes of the mover's life. It is the start of their coming to terms with events and learning some of the lessons of the experience.

VI Integration

The change event begins to become integrated within the overall features of the mover's life. A sense of its impact begins to grow. The wider opportunities within the situation, both

The Helper's Stages and Tasks

solution. The mover may need their doubts and uncertainties for some considerable time. This, however, does not mean that the process is going awry. Trust the mover and trust the process. Keep your own anxieties to yourself and help the mover deal with those of their own, rather than those you wish they would deal with.

V Managing the Change: Challenge and Support

This is the period when the helper can be most free in their response and offer whatever is needed. The mover has enough experience behind them to find the lessons, to confront their own exaggerated expectations and recognise the opportunities that they may be overlooking. A strong relationship between mover and helper can make an enormous difference at this stage.

VI Integration and Reflection

This is the time to help the mover review and assess where they stand; to begin to integrate where they may still go and what they may still wish to contribute by way of effort to the

Reaction Cycle for the 'Mover'

taken and lost, can be more easily acknowledged. Serious re-ordering is no longer possible, though small adjustments may take place.

The final stage of moving through a major transition is that of *making it mine,* of owning and clarifying the event, along with all its shortcomings and blessings. The person can now move on, the experience of this particular transition complete.

The Helper's Stages and Tasks

change event. It is important at this stage that the mover recognises that further efforts can only have a limited influence on the overall pattern that has developed. It is also important for the mover to begin to develop a realistic appraisal of what has been accomplished. This is much more valuable than feeding false hopes or idealised visions.

To be life-changing, to be a permanent transformation, integration has to take place. The new situation, the new way of being **becomes** the individual when integration has taken place.

VII Reflection and Evaluation

Only with the perspective of time, distance and the opportunity to reflect can the mover begin to evaluate the overall influence of the change within the events that make up their life. The job may now only be a job. The ending of the relationship may have brought important learning despite the accompanying hurt. The move to a new area may have brought problems not anticipated at the time, and so on.

VII Evaluation

The helper can now assist the mover to review the event more clearly, by holding up a mirror and supporting them as they take stock of what they see. The mover must begin to make sense of what has taken place and what the consequences suggest for the way ahead.

This final stage has to be worked with consciously. Only in rare cases will reflection and integration occur fully or without support and encouragement. People have to spend time and effort to gather the lessons of experience to themselves. All too often other events overtake us, crowding out the time we would like to give to reflection on past events.

The helper is able to encourage this reflection and give the mover the opportunity to help identify and own the changes, the consequences of those changes and to consider 'Where next'?

Summary

This framework is an outline only. It is not linked to any particular change event and so may be used as a guideline for many situations and events. Again, it should be stressed that not everyone will pass through the stages given, nor will individuals spend equal time passing through each phase. However, it will be useful to bear these stages and pointers in mind whilst working with anyone who is moving through the change process.

Chapter Fifteen

Helping the Dying and
Their Loved Ones

Death as Culmination and Fulfillment

In other cultures death was the culmination, the fitting end, the magnificent moment to be longed for and prepared for lovingly. Ceremony, ritual, art, religion all came together to provide a preparation for the soul's departure. By comparison we have so little.

As we meet death, the urge to understand, the need to know grows. We seek to find a meaning; a way of joining the threads of our life together to gain a sense of coherence, if not order, to our experience. Wanting to know what our life added up to, evaluating our accomplishments, these concerns are natural activities. Completing our affairs, making amends where possible, forgiving oneself and others, are all part of the process of finishing off, completing life, closing the shutters so that we can turn our attention inwards.

This process of closure can be a gradual, peaceful withdrawal, or a frantic fearful obsession to do the impossible or resist the inevitable. Recognising it as part of the process in whatever form it comes, enables helpers and friends become more prepared to do all they can to encourage the dying person to move through closure as well as is possible given all the contributing circumstances.

The Need for Courage

This requires a willingness to speak the unspeakable; to ask the *un-askable* and to risk getting it wrong. It means following the dying person's lead rather than saying things like *'I think you had better sort out your relationship with your brother'*. It means providing openings for the dying person to explore tentatively. It means being on the look out.

The dying person may be nervous of surfacing long held secrets, past events, hurts or even loving memories and need the gentle reassurance of others present who are willing to spend time beside them: time and more time to be there and for the dying person to return to those topics they need to discuss further.

They may need the help of others to explore religious or spiritual questions that take on new significance. They may seek new help to clarify their affairs. For some it will be an important time to complete dearly loved projects and ambitions; a last chance. For others there will be the struggle to go on with life until *My grandchild's fifth birthday* or *I see my daughter get married* and such people may hold on until the moment of their dying wish, only ready to leave once it has been accomplished.

Responding to the Dying

An individual's involvement in their own death depends upon their ability and their willingness to cope. Some people may want a great deal of responsibility, whilst others may show little interest or capacity to tackle the matter. The particular circumstance, too, has to be taken into account, whether it is a sudden realisation, for example, or the outcome of a prolonged struggle.

Responding to the individual and their needs is crucial, rather than assuming you know what they need. It is essential to spend time ascertaining what each individual's needs are and how best they might be met. We cannot simply assume we know. Checking out our assumptions continuously is crucial.

Both the type and the quality of an individual's support have to be considered. Not everyone is blessed with an understanding and loving family. The context of the relationships that make up an individual's life has to be seen for what it is. Last minute reconciliations do sometimes happen, but all too often the end happens in much the same way as the living has been.

It is important for the dying person to have an opportunity to gain as full a grasp as possible of where they are, if they are to recover those things they wish to make their own before they die. Recognising where they have come to in their life gives the person an opportunity to decide what else may be left to accomplish.

Acceptance does not mean giving up. It is not simply a question of recognising the end. It means opening up to the opportunities that still lie ahead in the time remaining. **The helper has to believe this too, if they are to encourage the dying person to believe and act upon it.**

Helping the Dying: Crisis and Closure

For those of us affected by the imminent loss of a loved one, facing sudden catastrophic news, or experiencing the pain of rejection from a broken relationship we do not want to lose, **the overwhelming feeling can be one of powerlessness in the face of the inevitable. Emptiness, numbness, panic, all form part of the reaction as we feel unable to respond usefully at all.**

When we are helping a loved one face death, all those feelings are there, as well as the desire to help and the anger at the future loss. It becomes impossible. to separate our own needs in the situation from those of our loved one. We are in danger then of behaving in ways that help us cope rather than meet the real wishes of the person dying. We then project on to the other person what we hope they need, but which in fact are those things which help us to function. And we often feel guilty as we do it. A feeling that somewhere in all this, it is not quite as we would like it to be, but somehow we are unable to know what else to do or how to do it.

Completion

Deeply loving relationships may sometimes, therefore, come to an end on a false note or a collusive pretence, when the patient plays the carer's game in order to make them feel better; all the time suffering because they cannot, or dare not raise the issues they need to have raised or resolved. The over co-operative patient and the solicitous helper together may collude to miss the vital moments of contact as the end draws near.

We all know too, of examples of the very opposite where imminent death has brought a crisis to a relationship that those involved have transcended. They then go on to discover a richer, deeper communion together that makes even death a blessing; for only a crisis of such scope and seriousness could be sufficient to put aside all the barriers and resentments previously in the way.

Counselling Relations of the Dying

Perhaps more than anything it is the need for a consistency of approach and information amongst all parties that is the most important aspect of care for the dying. Who knows what, when are essential considerations. Helpers need to face these issues with relatives and patients in sensitive yet clear ways in order that everyone knows the pattern of response that is being aimed at. Confusion and uncertainty are difficult enough at such periods without having the lack of any clear stance on behalf of the helpers themselves added to the circumstances. However, having said that, there are still too many situations which are far from satisfactory because the helping team have not been able to work out their own position.

Ensuring that family members are not caught in traps of not sharing information they desperately want to share is an important consideration for helpers. Helping people consider what they want in the way of information; what they want to do with it; what the implications are of whatever course of action may be chosen and then reviewing, *Is that what you intended?* forms part of the detached but concerned role of the helper. Helping people assume responsibility for the information they receive and how they use it, whilst providing space for referral to a counsellor to explore the impact if required is essential.

Vulnerability

Death brings us face to face with our own mortality, our vulnerability and our limits. We will not go on for ever and we will not be able to change it. How much we are attached to our body, our egos, our identities; how far we have the support of a spiritual understanding will greatly influence our response. In times of such vulnerability we are open to the manipulation, of going along with the wishes of others, simply because it's hard to know what we want, or to know what to do - the circumstances are so unprecedented and after all *'Helpers are supposed to know best. They are trained aren't they?'* So often at these critical times patients, relatives, friends, give up their involvement, handing themselves over to the skilled helper with a naive trust that it will all be managed for them - perhaps even painlessly too. Unable to face the awesomeness of all that is happening, it seems possible that the young woman in a uniform may have the answer.

Risks for the Helper

Helpers facing those so shattered, bereft or numbed by events may all too easily respond out of the best of intentions, implying that they do indeed know what is best and thus take over a situation that is only tragically simple on the surface. A helpful willingness to get drawn in too naively may be paid for by angry exchanges later when you didn't save the father, brother or little girl.

The assumption that you think for a moment that you do know what is needed may be your downfall, as the issues and complexities of the family history become more and more tangled into the issue of care and how best to manage it. And the guilt that you weren't doing enough, or should have done it differently is then never far away. And if you avoid all those temptations, it's still all too easy to misread a signal, misunderstand a request, or overlook someone's need, creating a setback in a painfully won relationship.

Helping the dying or the bereaved is such difficult work. But the reward, as those dedicated to it testify, is to be granted moments of such privileged intimacy into the life journey of another soul that all the hurt, anger and confusion are set to one side.

The Need for Inner Stillness

It is not work for everyone to take on. It may be that we know it is not our work and yet we may find ourselves there, in the situation, facing it with relatives or patients. We must then remember to find a place in ourselves where we can witness what is happening and do all we can to respond to the true needs of the situation. An important contribution is to help those who are living out the loss and death come to their own decisions, in their own way, whilst also recognising it is not always possible.

We must beware of hurrying people into decisions or prolonging the agony of indecision; of recommending actions that serve no real purpose or of hiding those things from those who wish to know. The dilemmas are endless and ever changing; support to share them is essential and all too rare in most cases.

The Need for Support and Supervision

Supervision, a place to more closely look inside how it was, what I did and how it affected me, with an experienced and trained colleague is essential. However, this is still practically non-existent for most helpers, who are thus condemned to struggle on responding in the only ways they know, long after they know there must be other ways.

This bleak picture is very slowly beginning to change. Support groups and patient groups are not as unusual as they were, even five years ago. Hospitals and social service departments are recognising that many people have no sizeable support system around them to deal with the kinds of issues that arise whether as professionals involved in this work, or as people living out the consequences of bereavement, grief and loss.

The Risk of Being 'Taken-Over'

Patient support is so rare. Over-helped in the beginning, our lives get overtaken by decisions provoked by experts, specialists and others, our grief can then be taken out of our hands as we are drawn along with events that cease in any vital respect to be 'ours' any more.

And for the helper aware of all this, the hardest struggle of all may be in realising the different ways colleagues believe things should be managed; of seeing the agony of the family; of wanting to respect and respond to its needs, but knowing that the human response may be seen as betrayal, or weakness, or lack of professionalism by colleagues who have decided on their 'policy'. A policy that all must abide by. And why is this? Because we have taken ourselves outside the domain of death - or tried to; because our way of life is based on the denial of death, on the assumption that we must all aspire to be young, vital and alive. We have created a culture which has no place for death and so we no longer know how to deal with it. And of course death won't go away.

The Difference Between Dying on One's Own and Dying Alone.

There are no travel plans for death, no holiday tour operators, no glossy brochures and no package deals. It is an individual journey. We may not die alone but we die on our own. It is a singular event; unrepeatable, unique and without benefit of rehearsals.

It is important that we do all we can to do the best for one another.

Chapter Sixteen

Supporting and Counselling the Bereaved

Bereavement

Bereavement is the least prepared for, hardest to accept and most universal experience of change, as the story of Buddha and the mustard seeds so well illustrates.

It is the loss of the person upon whom so many experiences and emotions are centred; pleasure, conflict, anxiety, love, anger. **It is simply the irretrievable loss of the familiar which puts the survivor beyond changing what they have said, done and felt.**

Commonly we experience the inability to sleep, exhaustion and loss of appetite. Symptoms are wide-ranging from headaches, rashes, chest pains, stomach illness, numbness and shock to emotional and psychological distress and loss of functioning. Forgetfulness, sudden outbursts of anger, or weeping in inappropriate and unexpected places, haunting memories and reminders, pervading apathy, aimlessness and futility accompanied by guilt and hostility to oneself and others in the search to find someone to blame, are all representative aspects. There are often times of seeking forgiveness from those present for supposed wrongs done to the dead person - a seeking of absolution, for supposed failings which are all too often exaggerated. Rarely is there any comfort when it is offered.

There are usually bouts of irritability and anger at those not suffering in the same way, who have not been so singularly chosen to suffer and this may lead to a repudiation of those previously important throughout the time of bereavement. Doctors, the church and helpers are often targets of such hostility.

Support and Counselling Through Grief and Loss

Not everyone who is bereaved needs counselling. All of us need support. Where we get it and what kind of support we need will vary.

Grief, too, we must always remember, is an individual journey. For many more than who seek it, a period of counselling to help with the bereavement and mourning would be immensely beneficial. However supportive friends are in the beginning, sooner or later they will expect or imply that it is time you moved on and you may not be ready. At this point it might be that the presence of a trained helper to offer space to explore feelings and reactions as much as is needed becomes a crucial resource.

This doesn't take away the importance of friends, but it helps ensure they are not over-strained in their patience and willingness, especially if they have any losses of their own to deal with.

Complex Grief

Sometimes a grief-reaction is so powerful, a death so apparently inexplicable or the circumstances so devastating that the natural process of grief is interrupted or distorted. The bereaved person gets 'stuck' and knows it. A constant picture of the event perhaps haunts them; a question they never asked torments them; guilt stalks their daily life and they are powerless to shake it off.

At such times the attention of a trained helper can be an invaluable source of support in helping to focus on the disturbance while not attempting to put the person right or 'get rid' of the grief. At such a time a helper is a guide through a sea of feelings, impressions and memories, able to provide a haven of stability. Such help may enable the bereaved person to gain more from what has been a time of pain and trial than they ever thought possible.

The space to recapture memories, celebrate moments, recall good times, bad times, reconnect with the past with a non-judgmental and accepting witness, can be so therapeutic and affirming. It is sad that all too few of us seek out the opportunity.

The writing which follows is one person's account of their journey through just such a complex reaction to grief. It highlights the value of having a trained helper accompany and be with someone going through this kind of transition.

I now know what it is like to live - but not be alive. With hindsight, awareness is easier. At the time of living it I was truly like a zombie. I was unaware of how I felt; unaware of the reality of my relationship with my husband; unaware of messages I was giving others - the opposite to my real needs; unaware of messages from childhood which controlled my life and which still have such powerful, unhelpful influences; unaware of an alternative to living in my head - to logically thinking things through.

I existed in a vacuum, but did not know it.

The sudden death of my husband in February 1991 precipitated a train of events which seemed to take on their own power. Almost a year later, I was thinking that I should be coping on my own. I was convinced other people would now be expecting me to be back to 'normal' but I didn't feel 'normal'. In fact I felt hellish. A weekend course in January 1992 proved to be the turning point in my life.

I began a journey that Spring. A journey I never even knew was possible or existed. A journey which has led me through many desperate, dark, fear and tear filled days. A journey which has led me to many insights, new awakenings - wonderful, magical moments alongside hard-hitting and sobering truths which are difficult to accept. This journey is still continuing, and always will.

There are still days when I wish I were dead, when I wish I could sink back into my pit of apathy, crawl back behind my wall. Not feeling; not hurting; not having to do anything; not to 'work' on me; not wanting to see anyone - but desperately not to feel anything. But these days are becoming fewer and fewer.

Above all, it is a journey I could never have travelled alone. When B offered to 'accompany' me on my journey I did not really know what he meant. I didn't know what lay in store for me. I did know I could not survive for much longer living the way I was. After our first session, I also knew I felt safe with him, accepted by him - this surprised me, I didn't think I was acceptable and I was so reluctant to show the 'real' me.

The battle had begun.

There seems to be three main strands to my journey:-

my head v my heart (my feeling being).

my physical and sexual being.

and my spiritual being.

At times one strand appeared more urgent, more desperate than another, but I am learning that they are strongly inter-linked and influence each other greatly. There seemed, at the time, absolutely no logic to the way certain issues would arise. The need to understand, to know, to see the logic in everything was very strong. I now believe this in itself determined the way the first sessions would go.

I had a powerful resistance to revealing feelings, to even owning to feelings - to their very existence.

There was such an internal conflict. I had an overpowering need at times to cry. A seemingly ever increasing need, yet I knew this to be wrong. Crying is a weakness, a loss of self-control. 'What on earth will others think if I cry, after all it's 12,18 months, 2 years ago since IT happened. Only people who can't cope cry and I can cope with anything - my mother keeps telling me this, so it must be true! And anyway, 'good' Christians don't need to cry because they should be able to use their faith to sustain them and gain serenity.

I was being encouraged to let go. Even in the first session I nearly ended in tears. All I felt was caring and compassion but my response was 'I should have more control. I promised myself I wouldn't cry.'

I didn't know how to 'let go'. Self-control was my prime directive. I did not know how to allow my feelings to just be. I did not know how to accept them, work with them and so move on. In many a session I would be so physically tense to prevent emotional relaxation as well - the feared tears. I feared what would happen if I really did let go. What would I say; what would I do; what would I look like; what would B REALLY think of me then. Fear of rejection was huge. Fear of being laughed at was equally huge.

In one of the first sessions, when he was quietly, lovingly encouraging me to let go he told me, 'This house is well used to tears, including mine'. Those last two words have had a prolonged and deep influence on me. Did he really show his feelings in this way? Even more, did he really not mind me knowing that? Those words have been with me many, many times.

Over many sessions I began to see that B was in a totally different place. Tears were not a threat to him. They were not even signs of weakness. They were not to be avoided or scorned. He was not judging me. All the judgements, all the 'shoulds' and 'oughts' were from me. 'I should have more control'. 'I should not need to cry'. 'I ought to be able to think all this through logically'. He began to tell me when I was judgemental. I never realised how often I would put myself down or castigate myself for the way I was feeling at that moment.

This continued - and still does! And I began to be aware of what I said and more to the point how I seemed to judge everything black or white. And it was becoming apparent that I had one rule for me and another one for everyone else. It is OK for others to cry. It is OK for others to show anger etc - but not for me. I should be able to control them.

For the first time in my life I felt accepted totally. Accepted in spite of the tears, in spite of the anger, in spite of the hate, in spite of the weaknesses I perceived in the way I cried in sessions and on the 'phone. It was this acceptance, the love shown to me, which enabled me to begin a shift in my perception of me. I was no longer fighting B but fighting myself. A conflict between taboos from childhood and a new way I was beginning to see.

This way means honesty. Honesty with myself as to how I am feeling. This way means accepting how I feel, allowing it to be, allowing my feelings to teach me the way forward. I began to allow my feelings to show. There was still the fear of being completely consumed by the power of the emotions. I had come to realise that the sadness and the tears were only part of the fear of feelings. There were other, even less acceptable feelings lurking under the surface. Anger, hatred, and jealousy were all there waiting to consume me. I was frightened - no, terrified - of allowing these free reign. The power they had. The strength of feeling I had never, never experienced before. How could I control them. How could I keep pushing them down and pretend they didn't exist? The answer to both of course, was that if I wanted to learn anything, if I simply wanted to survive, then I couldn't.

Pushing down and denying these feelings was taking all my energy. By this time I was existing on nervous energy - my physical stores had long been used up. Work became an endurance test. My training for fitness was becoming obsessional. Being with people, pretending to be OK was nigh impossible - yet I couldn't bear to be on my own. Running no longer kept the anger, the hatred, the bitterness or the guilt at bay as it had for so long. Physically, I was becoming weaker and since this was one area of my life in which I had confidence and some pride it was the final straw. I went to the doctors, I thought I had a chest infection, only to fall to pieces when he asked how I was. 'What a wimp' was my internal reaction - I couldn't even hide my feelings anymore. In retrospect, I know this was the best thing that could have happened. I was signed off work and remained so for over three months.

I remember little of this time. It was an enormous effort to get up, to wash and dress. I lived in a dark pit from which there seemed no escape. The fear, the despair, the loneliness, the strength of feelings seemed to possess me totally day in and day out. There was a feeling of having lost everything. A feeling of total emptiness and blackness.

I do remember feeling selfish because I concentrated on how I was feeling with little thought for others. Writing was important. I often sent notes I had written after time spent in my study. It was somehow easier to put embarrassing or frightening things onto paper and work from there in the next session. Other strategies included ways of breaking the ties between me and Neil and me and mother; writing letters (to Neil) and painting. This last one caused me problems. I was furious with him when he suggested this. After all, I'm colour blind so there was absolutely no point in using colour! However, he insisted and he also said I would have to take them to him because I wouldn't know what they meant. Eventually, I began to realise it was fear of revealing yet more of the 'real' me instead of the masks and the colour blindness was an excuse.

Many of those feelings, parts of the 'real' me, were really not acceptable. They are negative. They are definitely not Christian and certainly 'nice' people don't have them. The concept of my 'shadow side' was alien to me. I began to learn of my shadow side. Over time I began to accept it is part of being human, truly human and alive.

Small things would lead to me losing my temper, not being able to handle everyday mishaps, over-reacting to situations in school. I was 'leaking' all over the place - usually in inappropriate places. When not acknowledged, not expressed, they remain laying in wait, waiting for any excuse to appear. I hesitantly and reluctantly began to accept the truth of this. To even acknowledge their presence seemed wrong. How dare I say that I hated Neil. How dare I say I was angry with him. How dare I say I hated my mother? How could I say that I was jealous of those who still had their partners; jealous of those with loving families?

There was so much fear. Fear, again, of what would happen if I really lost control and said EXACTLY what I wanted to. Fear of rejection. I took the risk. There is one session where I remember very little except that I ranted and raved about Neil. About the way he had treated me, about the way we had lived and about the way he had contributed to his own death. This in itself was progress of a kind because prior to this I had blamed everybody - God, me, the company he worked for - anyone except recognising that Neil's lifestyle, his very 'make-up' had been the major influence on the shortness of his life. There were occasions when B was very blunt - almost forceful - in pointing this out to me. Forceful - yes, but always accepting and non-judgemental. I needed that bluntness to shake me out of self-pity. To shake me out of the guilt I was 'crucifying' myself with.

Since reading books I begin to see he was (and is) operating from a stance of 'I'm OK, You're OK' whilst I work from 'I'm not OK, You're OK'. (This is an on-going issue.) As part of my movement to 'I'm OK, You're OK', he frequently used a phrase which eventually began to make sense - 'Be a witness and not a judge', (of my own actions and feelings). What a difference this has made. I'm still learning this but it is so different, so releasing, so empowering.

Perhaps you're wondering why I have placed so much emphasis on this 'strand' of my journey. It was so fundamental to the development of the relationship within the sessions: fundamental to the awareness I was gaining into living in my heart as well as my head; into the trust I had in the safety of my 'protected' space; in his understanding - he's been there. His acceptance and non-judgemental attitude was crucial in approaching an even more impossible area for me. It has been important to me knowing that his comments, challenges, strategies, interventions were not based on purely theoretical knowledge and training.

It was through the development of this relationship that I began to be willing to talk about the dreams I was having. I knew them to be disgusting, obscene and an indication of the kind of person I was. And, let's face it, if anyone else knew what I was dreaming then they would not want to know me. I had been brought up to believe that 'nice' people don't talk about such things. Nice people, especially ladies, do not talk about the body, never reveal it except to a marriage partner. Through many discussions concerning the implanting of messages; reading books on sexual issues and life scripts I began to realise how repressed and suppressed I had been and still was as an adult.

The single most important factor in enabling me to begin to let go, after his acceptance, was his own open attitude. He talked freely, using words which made me cringe just hearing them. With encouragement, an increasing sense of safety and a knowledge that in every other perceived risk that I had taken my fears had proved to be groundless, I began to tell some of the dreams. What a weight off my mind. B offered a totally different perspective. Perhaps I wasn't so depraved and so obscene after all. The process of truly accepting this in my heart took well over a year. It is only since that stage that I am now able to work more on what it means to be a woman - to be female as against some asexual being I was brought up to be.

One of the things I have missed so very much since Neil died is physical contact with other human beings. I had believed I was OK. I didn't need any contact other than with Neil. All I did know was that I was desperate for something I had no means of getting. B suggested - no he didn't, he told me - to go for a massage. I had never heard of anything so ridiculous. How dare he suggest such a thing. I think I knew that if I relaxed physically I would not be able to keep up the masks, I would not be able to stay behind my 'wall'. Finally, I agreed but only with someone I knew. The first session was hell. Getting undressed was purgatory but the whole session was handled with sensitivity and respect. I never knew how much my body can tell me about all kinds of things. Being able to feel physically was so different. During this time I had also discovered that some of my friends were equally accepting and loving. I was able to continue work begun in massage or with B with them. It was becoming clearer to me that it was me giving all the judgements, me giving me a very hard time indeed. Their support and willingness to listen, to just be there has been invaluable.

Previously, I have compartmentalised everything - physical energy, nervous energy, emotional energy and sexual energy. I now realise they are all part of one whole. I was denying myself access to a tremendous source of energy. This meant that I was not living fully and that I limited the possibilities for my growth.

I would stay with one issue long after I had really worked through it because it felt safe. Even if it was hellish - at least I knew the issue; I knew where I was. Letting go of one thing inevitably meant dealing with something else. I had no husband; didn't have an identity anymore; the illusions of a loving caring childhood had disintegrated; illusions concerning my marriage had gone; all my foundations were under severe threat. So much change, so much lost. Letting go took courage and a lot of support and energy. I can still catch myself doing this - an avoidance of moving on.

Throughout the whole of this time, I had relied very heavily on the faith I had as a Christian. Even at my darkest time - in the Pit - I did not feel deserted by God. At least I still had that. The strong, tangible presence of God the first night after Neil's death remains with me still. Yet, in other ways my beliefs were a handicap to me. Many were inherited from childhood. These had a straitjacket effect on the way I viewed things. Early in my journey, guilt was so strong that I could see absolutely no possibility of ever being forgiven and certainly never forgiving myself. A comment made by B shocked me almost into a new way of looking at this. The conversation went something like this:- 'I don't know much about theology. But I thought it was Christ crucified for the world? Not Christ crucified for the world, except you!' This made me aware of another dimension, a spiritual one, which was to run alongside and through everything else. I was frequently brought back to it by being asked 'Where was God in all this?' I am fortunate in having a priest (and friend) who has been equally accepting, non-judgemental and willing to be with me in my searchings for and against God. During services, when I was more open, generally more vulnerable, I came to be aware of God quietly but firmly telling me to let go of everything. Not to hold anything back. The more I hung onto the past, the more I clung to issues I found hard, the less room there was for him. Less room for God to move in and simply take over. But there was still the 'losses' if I did this - of support, of hugs when I was upset; of safety in the known. I well remember B saying he was looking forward to the time when he could sit back and watch me drown. I was angry - I already felt as if I was drowning, but I had misunderstood. Drown -yes- but in God's love. I was to remember this a long time after it was said. So, I ran away from God, except at the times it was convenient to me!

The insights I was gaining through massage, through energy work, I found strange but exhilarating. I was experiencing things I never knew existed. I was finding I was far less judgemental, after all I didn't know what was going to happen next. These were happening to me, not some erudite theologian or academic or some 'way-out' sixties hippie! I could open my mind, my heart to God. This process so far had taken something over 15 months. Then, something happened which altered everything. A comment made in a session about the veracity of parts of the Bible and I was thrown into utter despair. I lost everything. I had no God. The one thing which had sustained me, the thing I felt had kept me from committing suicide, the one lifeline through the Pit, through the months of pain and agony. That was gone. I felt destroyed. Why that? Now, I had absolutely nothing left. WHY had he deserted me? I know what it's like to feel to be in hell. I think I can now understand something of the desperation leading to suicide. It was only the hours spent by B talking me through it, the hours with my priest that enabled me to survive intact. 'This is your "crucifixion" and after that is the resurrection'. 'You had faith in your faith'. This I did not understand, but now is becoming much clearer and is accurate.

A change began about a week later. I was early for a massage session and I went into the site of a ruined Abbey. No plan for that and I still don't know how that trip was so quick to give me the time to visit the Abbey. There was an irresistible urge to kneel there on the stone floor. The sun shone through onto me. One question I asked - 'What more do you want from me'. The answer was clear and firm, but said in love - 'Everything'. 'Then I can begin to fill you'. I now realised that anything I put between myself and God would be taken away. Not long ago I would have said this kind of experience didn't happen to people like me.

This was the turning point. I KNEW that I had not been permanently deserted. The desert (as I came to think of it) was instrumental in heralding the next and most exiting stage so far in my journey. All my foundations, all my values and beliefs were under threat - but I knew God was there A fantastic feeling of being surrounded by God, in his love - that drowning B had spoken of? One especially vivid and lasting feeling when I was at the top of a mountain, freezing cold and in thick mist! Then, I had a magical 3 weeks in August 1993.

As all three strands of my journey continue to weave in and out of each other they feel as though they are becoming more at one. With less separation between them, it feels as though I am becoming more at one - with myself and with God. There are many marvellous times when the penny drops - when realisation dawns - often about something I've struggled with for ages; something which B has been telling me about for ages. Yet, there are still times when I feel lost; times when I feel distraught; times when I feel I have to speak to someone - hear a friendly voice or go insane.

So many things have changed. I have only recently begun to see this as the changes were rarely conscious decisions but which happened as part of the whole process.

I eat different foods.

My weight is much more as I wish it and more stable.

I dress differently.

I SEE things differently - things look clearer, sharper, different.

I listen differently.

I know I'm less judgemental and hard.

I'm far more open to different experiences.

Even a medical problem, (stress related they say) I've taken medication for years is different.

I look different - if what many people say is to be believed.

I trust my feelings so much more than I did.

I have left my career of 24 years.

My colour vision is much improved.

I have great difficulty at times accepting all this. Is this really me? Is this a permanent transformation or a temporary high spot which will go when I'm no longer in the environment where this kind of spiritual journey is actively sought after and encouraged?

I KNOW I can fly - but my wings feel very small and inexperienced. I wish, more than anything else I can think of, to continue this journey. I wish to learn so much more about the concepts and issues I have touched on in the last 2 years. A journey which I now know was essential for me to undertake in order to begin to develop into a whole, feeling human being, but one which has not been easy and could not have been done alone.

Heather Tweddle

The Helper's Task Through the Mourning Period

Helping and counselling are not the same thing and many bereaved people, as we have already stated, would neither seek counselling nor need it. They will, however, need help. The helper must first consider the limits of their role. However much the heart opens to the suffering of another, the very nature of the work they undertake will set limits on how far any helper can go in whatever type and level of help they offer.

This may well create difficulties of role management and create role conflict. The needs of the situation may be such that you wish to respond more fully than your role allows. Living with the pain of such circumstances is not easy. Help for the helpers is essential in raising the implications of such human dilemmas. Nevertheless, it is no answer to befriend every bereaved client.

Sometimes the nature of the contact between helper and the bereaved person is of a short duration - a short hospital stay for example - and the meetings together

127

may be relatively few. The relationship may be much more crucial to the bereaved family than to the helper. It may be on the strength of practically no contact at all that the helper has to confront someone with devastating news. These are just some of the many and difficult challenges any helper may have to face when working with people in mourning or who are bereaved.

It is important in the initial stages to work out how far and for how long a helper can be available. Then, at an appropriate moment, begin to make the conditions of your availability clear so that people begin to know that you are not here all day, every day. Your job is to help them manage themselves and where they can't, to find the next point of referral to other, more skilled and specialist help, if need be. Share the dilemmas rather than attempt to carry them alone. And remember, people don't have to get anywhere. They need time to feel where they are more than anything else.

If you find the idea of the bereaved wanting to talk to the person who has died morbid, do not get involved and do not be judgmental about it - either of the client or yourself. You may have to remember just how much you too have talked to people from your past who matter to you.

Many mourners feel the fear of judgement about what are perfectly natural processes like talking to the dead person; feeling their presence around them; being overcome with sudden memories; unbidden reminders; the cycling inter-play of feelings. **If, as a helper you can only pretend it is alright because you aren't at home with such processes yourself you will not help, you will get in the way.**

Whilst helping people manage themselves does mean enabling them to function in their day to day life, it doesn't mean jollying them along and trying to get them to look on the *bright side* in order to make you feel happy. It means giving useful attention to day-to-day life, along with the other activities that make up the complex process that is mourning.

Chapter Seventeen

Grief Work

Mourning and Bereavement

In his book **'Grief Counselling and Grief Therapy'** William Worden explains that there are four major tasks each of us has to accomplish when dealing with a bereavement. These tasks do not have to be taken in sequence and we can be working at any one of them and having an effect upon others, but the four areas of concern have to be successfully resolved before we are able to move on into the rest of our lives.

They are:
- **To make actual the reality of the loss itself.**

- **To experience the pain of grief.**

- **To make adjustments to the fact that the dead person is no longer present.**

- **To withdraw our emotional energy from the past relationship and into new ones.**

To Make Actual the Reality of the Loss.

It is one thing for someone to know that their partner has died or that a child has been killed in a road accident; it is quite another for the impact of such a devastating event to filter fully into consciousness. The actual reality of such a major loss has to be given time to make itself felt; with all the attendant turbulence, false hope, disbelief and denial that will be involved.

To Experience the Pain of Grief.

The grieving process is long and complex. It involves violent switches in mood and preoccupation, changing thoughts; sudden forgetfulness and painfully obsessive recollections. It is often accompanied by feelings of guilt about the part the individual has played in the relationship of the past and a desire to have done more - a usually unrealistic desire. For many there is a sense of *'This shouldn't be happening to me'* or *'I should be more in control than I am'*.

The pain of grief is hard and long and it is in no one's interest to foreshorten it or try to make things better by pointing out it will all be better one day. For the person grieving, there is only an endless sense of the prolonged and enduring pain of the present.

To Adjust to the Fact That the Dead Person is No Longer There.

The loss of any important relationship, however much anticipated, through illness or the process of separation brings with it many unexpected consequences which have to be lived through without any preparation. There are the occasions when a fleeting memory suddenly arises; when a piece of music recalls a special memory or when walking by a street reawakens something from the past.

In addition there may be the daily reminders of how much a space now exists with the loved one gone for ever. Living through this period is often experienced as extremely isolating. Although many people know that others would be interested in their welfare they often feel unable to face the awkwardness of meeting. After a while the avoidance of contact can become a very real problem keeping the grieving person locked further into the mourning process.

Withdrawing Emotional Energy and Putting it Into New Relationships.

Life moves on but for the bereaved relative there may be little interest or energy in finding a place in it for a long time. They may exist in a mental and emotional limbo; finding the motivation to do anything more than take care of themselves impossible. Sometimes even these rudimentary routines break down and the person gives way to an inward collapse.

Moving on into a new life may need a lot of gentle persuasion and sometimes such persuasion can be used to reject the giver as well as the advice. It is often difficult for those close to a bereaved person to know just how much encouragement and exhortation to offer. In so many ways, they can never get it right.

It may be a long time before the bereaved person is ready to begin the slow re-adjustment to take up a new role and status in life and to begin to build new relationships that reflect their changed position. And for the grieving person all the old relationships from the past take on a new dimension - at least for a time; something others tend to forget. It may seem that John is still John, but John is now a widower and that brings a new aspect to his identity and sense of self. These adjustments take time.

The Need for Understanding on the Part of the Helper

In addition to the skills and qualities of becoming a useful helper, part of any helper's effectiveness lies in the understanding they can enable the client to gain in the work done together. How far the helper understands the issues of relationships, the stages of transition, the processes of mourning and so on, will influence how far the client responds and what the client learns.

To be effective, a helper needs to be aware of such issues as:-

- **How does the individual presently make sense of what has happened?**

- **Is the loss intelligible, given their view of the world?**

- **Can any purpose be derived from the event?**

- **How ambiguous or conflicted was the meaning of what has been lost?**

- **What interpretation of loss would the individual's underlying structure of meaning be likely to support?**

- **How do the person's present circumstances and relationships affected by the loss support or frustrate the effective working out of the grieving process?**

This aspect of the helping process is often left to take care of itself. The argument seems to go that with enough help of the right kind, time and the healing process itself will be sufficient for things to work out. This is not necessarily so.

People can move through major changes at an emotional level and still be left with things incomplete because they have not enlarged their understanding about what has happened to them or found useful ways to integrate their experience into their growth and development as people.

What follows is not written as an encouragement for helpers to supply ready-made world-views to clients in need. It must be emphasised that the process of clarification and reassessment will only be successful if the helper has developed an understanding of the processes of change and loss from out of their own life experience and, as a result, is secure enough within their own frame of reference to allow the client to establish a sense of meaning for themselves. The growth and enlargement of personal meaning is perhaps the greatest neglected gift of the counselling process when working with loss and change.

Working With the Bereaved

An important feature in the helping process of working with the grieving or the bereaved is allowing the client to take the time to adjust to the actuality of the loss. This is not something necessarily straightforward or accomplished at one moment.

There are times when the person in mourning may well forget the trauma ever happened. They may well *know* that it happened but at another level they are too benumbed by the impact to fully register it as a part of the continuous flow of their lives.

These moments of forgetfulness can be extremely disturbing to the bereaved who may well feel that they are losing their grip on life.

Working with Feelings

Helping the client to identify and express the often confusing range of feelings that make up the grieving process is complex work. The feelings often shift and are seemingly contradictory. They are powerful and often of a kind that the client feels sure would be disapproved of socially. The naturally accompanying negative feelings that go with any serious loss are amongst the most difficult to surface and to express. But if they are held onto for too long then the client may find themselves at the mercy of unsuccessful attempts at self-control which only make them even more distressed at their inability to cope.

The major sources of difficult feelings to work with are:-

Anger.

Anger is an inevitable part of grief and there are many, many sources of it in the grieving process. Just one example is when it may actually have been a blessing for an ageing relative to die with dignity, but you may well still feel abandoned. Anger will recur at varying points, often at what seem, to the person who is grieving, to be inexplicable moments. It is likely to be very strong and there will be the fear of being consumed or overwhelmed by it. The triggers may appear to be trivial, leaving the person grieving with no real sense of the focus of the anger - yet the anger is very real and very powerful.

The effective helper needs to allow the person to express this anger without seeking justification for it. If the helper is not comfortable with this depth and strength of feeling, then this will be transmitted and the freedom to express the anger will be denied.

Guilt.

However much loved they were, the person who has died had their fair share of imperfections and shortcomings. You did not have them all. It cannot all be your fault. A common feeling of the bereaved is that they somehow didn't do all that they could and that because the death has happened at all, it must be someone's fault and someone must be to blame. These are common and unrealistically exaggerated feelings. Sometimes, of course, there are elements of truth in them and we are brought face to face with our own selfishness or pettiness. Helping someone to distinguish between appropriate and inappropriate guilt is extremely important.

Anxiety.

It is common to experience a sense of being unable to cope, of feeling overwhelmed by even the smallest of details and a sense of morbid pointlessness. Agitation and restlessness, the need to find things to do and yet to get no comfort from them, the endless ruminating and losing track are all part of the anxiety of dislocation and discontinuity which take place at a time of serious loss. This is a period when a person's anchor points are under threat, undergoing the process of change, as they come to terms with the overall impact of their loss. Anxiety is usually a prolonged period in the process of grieving following immediate trauma.

It is essential that the helper encourages acceptance of the feelings around anxiety; acceptance that it is OK to be uncertain; that is OK to 'not know' or they will become anxious about their anxiety and compound the issue. It is not, however, part of the helper's role to provide false reassurances or to become exaggeratedly concerned - it is important to be steady and reassuring in order to enable the person who is grieving to express their feelings freely in this area. It is likely that the helper is providing the only space where such feelings can be safely expressed.

Sadness.
It is important *to be present* and to allow the need for crying and mourning to happen and to both encourage and allow the release of feeling. It is also important to encourage the person to free themselves from the constraints of time limits - either self-imposed or as a result of perceived pressure from society to 'be over it'. Each person will move through this phase at different speeds, in different ways and will revisit it at different times. There is no right or wrong length of time for the need for tears or mourning, only the time that is needed.

Differences Between Depression and Grief

Depression differs from grief in that:-

'Grief expresses the intense anxiety and despair that the disintegration of meaning provokes, while depression represents a perverse re-integration, where worthlessness is conceived in order to make sense the futility.' (Marris P. xi)

It is as though the very natural feeling of helplessness, which is so much a part of the grieving process, the feeling that nothing seems worth doing because for a time at least it seems all meaning has gone, becomes generalised to the point where life itself begins to seem meaningless. Nothing seems worth doing and there seems nothing important enough to do. In normal grieving, the state of despair is itself an important impulse which provokes the restless search to recover meaning. However, in grief-related depression, the despair becomes the focus for rationalisation and the justification for things remaining hopeless. The findings in a study by George Brown and Tirrill Harris into the causes of depression suggest that:-

'.... depression commonly occurs when feelings of helplessness become diffused and associated with a sense of worthlessness. The insecurity of childhood attachments, stressfulness of present circumstances, the lack of emotionally supportive relationships and some precipitating loss or misfortune combine to

overwhelm the victim's hopes in life. But instead of providing a restless search to recover a sense of purpose, as in normal grief, the despair is contained by a self-defeating rationalisation'. (In Marris Pp xi-xii)

Bereavement, Attachment and Social Change

The experience of bereavement, the loss of a loved one, undermines our trust in our previous attachments. The knowledge, ability and sense of self-worth that we have struggled to achieve thus far, and which is in part invested in the loved one we have lost, has now gone. It is this experience that creates the condition for that sense of futility and hopelessness which is the initial characteristic of grief.

Bereavement robs us of a crucial attachment and disrupts our ability to organise experience. In just the same way social changes which disrupt our ability to interpret or respond to our world of experience bring about similar reactions.

'Both call for a process of recovery whereby the underlying structure of emotion and purpose can disengage itself from irretrievable assumptions, and circumstances without losing its ability to generate meaning'. (Marris P.x)

Implications

What is written above has implications for the training and preparation of a successful helper. Some understanding of personal change, a knowledge of the effects of loss and grief, a recognition of the impact of social change and a realisation that organisations are also in turbulence would seem a minimum for any helper.

Increasingly, individuals experience the effects of change at a personal level which may well have its origins in political or organisational change. Indeed, a major source of stress at work is the taking on of responsibility by individuals for what are the failures and mismanagement of the organisation to comprehend the consequences of the changes they are pursuing and their determined refusal to acknowledge the effects such changes have upon their workforce.

Organisational stress then becomes compounded with personal stress to give the individual an increasing sense of being 'to blame' for what is seen as a failure to cope. Of course this is the very situation many helpers feel themselves to be in.

Helpers in Need

Helpers, working in either the statutory or voluntary sector, are very likely themselves to be experiencing similar pressures and to be coping with less than ideal circumstances in which to do their work. The frequent consequence of this state of affairs is for the helper to become overloaded and this too needs to be challenged. *How far is my helping done at my own expense?*

How far do I use clients as an excuse for not looking after my own needs, or for not attempting to do something to improve the situation to benefit future clients? Such questions are not easy to answer.

Many of the established helping professions are themselves undergoing a massive re-definition of structure and purpose, leaving many experienced practitioners unsure of the value of their past contribution and deeply uncertain of their future role. In addition, we must not forget that helping is an ambiguous activity at the best of times. All helpers have mixed motives for the work they do, motives which they are not always aware of, or which they would like to admit to if they were.

Section III
Recommended Reading

Dass, R & Gorman, P	*How Can I Help* OP - considering reprint	
Kopp, S	*If You Meet The Buddha On The Road* Sheldon Press	1972
Lefebure	*Conversations On Counselling* T & T Clark, Edinburgh	1985
Taylor, B	*Working With Others* OASIS Publications	1987

Chapter Eighteen

Summary and Conclusion

Summary

Introduction

Section I began by examining the many changes taking place in our world today, the rate at which they are happening and the major influence they will have in respect to how we perceive what is happening to us now and how we feel about the future.

This led to an exploration of aspects of loss, grief and bereavement. The many complex issues surrounding death and attitudes towards death in our society are identified and examined. The ways in which individuals may receive traumatic news and their forms of response are also identified and explored. Reactions to loss, grief and bereavement in their varied forms are described in order to enable helpers be as effective as possible.

Section III concentrated on the ways in which helpers can be most effective in their role of helping someone through change. Those tasks and elements that it is important for the helper to be aware of and which are inherent in the process of change are highlighted and discussed.

What follows is a summary of this section. It is offered with the aim of enabling anyone involved in helping others through change to be as 'real' and effective as they are able.

Rights of the Dying

'Rights of the dying' here is meant to indicate the great importance of the considerations listed below. All need to be taken into account - not necessarily acted upon. The importance of having a list such as this is that helpers can then be aware of any signals the patient, or the dying person, offers to approach any of these areas of questioning. Again, it is worth emphasising it is their death not the helper's or the hospital's. The patient has a right to have **their** death as near to the way they choose as it is humanly possible to manage.

- **The consistency of what and how information is given, and the approach taken, is perhaps the most important consideration in helping the dying.**

- **Allow the individual access to the most accurate information about time, level of pain, nature of the end and management of death that they can understand and work with at the time (this will vary at different stages).**

- Encourage and answer all matter-of-fact questions, especially those which arise out of fear.

- Encourage the emergence of the person's feelings about dying as such, parting and what may lie beyond.

- Give space and support for catharsis (the discharge of any powerful feelings) followed by discussion.

- Encourage questions about the nature of the person's beliefs about what lies beyond and any spiritual needs they may wish to examine.

- Encourage bringing to a satisfactory close any unfinished emotional business with relatives and friends.

- Assist in directing attention to the management of any remaining practical affairs.

- Help with action planning for any special wishes or projects. 'What do I want to do with the time I have got left?'

- On repeat visits allow time and space for all the foregoing to occur as and when appropriate.

Counselling Relatives of the Dying

- Give, from the earliest opportunity, relevant information in suitable detail that the individual can cope with. This will vary from person to person and over time.

- Encourage, prepare and 'coach' relatives in how to deal with the patient's factual questions.

- Encourage the release of the relatives' feelings about the death of the patient.

- Encourage the relatives' exploration of their beliefs about death and the beyond and any spiritual concerns they may have.

- Encourage the relatives to be sensitive to the patient's need to deal with personal affairs and complete any special tasks in the time remaining.

- Alert the relatives to the need to say good-bye positively and to share and nurture the patient before their departure.

- Support relatives and encourage them if they need permission to be openly emotional with the patient.

Helping the Bereaved

- Help the bereaved acknowledge the loss and give support.

- Help the client move beyond the immediacy of the situation as and when appropriate.

- Help the client identify the role, tasks and practical affairs which are requiring attention.

- Help the person explore the need for grieving and periods of reminiscence, to remember anniversaries, special moments, events that trigger feelings and small incidents that trigger old, but loving memories.

- Many people have a phase where they think they are going crazy, because they believe they should not be acting the way they are. Reassurance is important at this stage.

- Offer reassurance that it is alright to feel 'that I don't always know what is happening' and give permission for the person to feel confused on occasion, or find themselves strangely moved by unexpected incidents and reminders from the past.

- Allow exploration and withdrawal of emotional attachment from the deceased, when signalled by the mourner. Some people need to stay attached longer than others. Some may simply need reassurance that it is okay to move on with life.

- Offer reassurance about new relationships and watch for the signs of too intense or too serious involvements beginning too soon, or which may be replacements or substitutions for the dead person.

- Respect individual differences.

- Ensure the continuity of support.

- Consider the individual's defences and their coping style, remembering that they need them.

- Seek specialist help if uncertain; but check first. Intervention by another helper can create an exaggerated fear of something being wrong on the part of the bereaved and complicate the situation.

Support and Counselling Through Grief and Loss

- Encourage the person to describe the past and the critical scenes over and over as often as they need to.

- Encourage the person to give literal descriptions of the critical scenes in the present tense as if they were happening now.

- Encourage the person to 'amplify' the experiences they offer to discuss and encourage the release of feelings.

- Encourage the person to speak 'directly' to the person who has died, to say whatever remains unsaid.

- Encourage them to write letters or speak to photographs.

- Invite the person to celebrate the qualities of the dead person, or describe shared moments in detail.

- Give support through the expression and release of feelings, including:-

Anger: the dead person may be better off but how does that leave the bereaved feeling?

Guilt: remind the person that they did all they could (if this is true). Guilt is often more acceptable than anger. People often feel guilty for feeling angry.

Sadness: help with the need to mourn and cry to gain release. Give permission for such feelings and reassurance that they are positive.

- Help seek the anger as well as the grief. There may be exaggerated fears of expressing irrational anger and negative feelings.

- Encourage the person to purge any redundant guilt through laughter.

- Encourage the person to repeat and stick to emotionally charged statements or phrases.

- Offer physical support and holding - without smothering.

- Bring the person back into the present time by positively anticipating actions or events ahead.

- Help them to gain positive direction for life ahead.

Conclusion

Working with the processes of change, loss and grief is a challenging field. Time and time again the helper has to realise *I am making assumptions* and go back to an earlier question, or an earlier phase in the work.

We may all go through similar events but we all go through them in individual and particular ways. Helping others understand their own individual processes and helping them work out what they can learn for themselves, rather than assuming we know the way they have gone through it and what they ought to learn, is an essential part of helping people in this area of work. Generating a space for others to meet themselves more fully and from that meeting, move on to what they are going to be in the future is always a more worthwhile, exciting and enriching task than telling people what you think they should know and how they ought to be - because it leaves the way open for you to be surprised too.

References

Lievegoed, B	*Phases* Rudolf Steiner Press	1979
Marris, P	*Loss And Change* RKP	1986
Sheehy, G	*Passages*	1989
Kubler Ross, E	*On Death And Dying* MacMillan	1969
McLuhan, M	*The Gutenburg Galaxy* Penguin	1963
Worden, W	*Grief Counselling And Grief Therapy* Springer, New York	1982